S0-AQL-377

# THE CONSUMMATION OF SOMETHING *Miraculous*

Jesus' Trials and Triumph of Redemption
A Study of Luke 16:19–24:53

BIBLE STUDY GUIDE

From the Bible-teaching ministry of

Charles R. Swindoll

INSIGHT FOR LIVING

Chuck graduated in 1963 from Dallas Theological Seminary, where he now serves as the school's fourth president, helping to prepare a new generation of men and women for the ministry. Chuck has served in pastorates in three states: Massachusetts, Texas, and California, including almost twenty-three years at the First Evangelical Free Church in Fullerton, California. His sermon messages have been aired over radio since 1979 as the *Insight for Living* broadcast. A best-selling author, Chuck has written numerous books and booklets on many subjects.

Based on the outlines and transcripts of Chuck's sermons, the study guide text is coauthored by Bryce Klabunde, a graduate of Biola University and Dallas Theological Seminary. He also wrote the Living Insights sections.

**Editor in Chief:**
Cynthia Swindoll

**Coauthor of Text:**
Bryce Klabunde

**Assistant Editor:**
Wendy Peterson

**Copy Editors:**
Deborah Gibbs
Glenda Schlahta
Karene Wells

**Text Designer:**
Gary Lett

**Publishing System Specialist:**
Bob Haskins

**Director, Communications and Marketing Division:**
Deedee Snyder

**Marketing Manager:**
Alene Cooper

**Project Coordinator:**
Colette Muse

**Production Manager:**
John Norton

**Printer:**
Sinclair Printing Company



ISBN 0-8499-8628-1
COVER DESIGN: Gary Lett
COVER PAINTING: *The Ascension* by Rembrandt van Rijn
Courtesy SuperStock, Inc.
Printed in the United States of America

# CONTENTS

# INTRODUCTION

In this final section of Luke's gospel, we'll witness the bittersweet moment when Christ's agony on the cross accomplished the finished work of our salvation.

As terrible and wonderful as that news is, though, the story doesn't end there. After the Crucifixion came the *Resurrection*. And without the Resurrection and the Ascension that followed, Jesus would have remained just another martyr for another worthy cause, the dead founder of another world religion. When Jesus rose from the dead, however, He became the lone conqueror of death, the triumphant Savior over sin, the ever-living Lord of all, our ever-present advocate before the Father.

Satan's doom was sealed, sin's ransom had been paid in full, and God's redemption plan was once-for-all, eternally secured. The miracle that began with Jesus' birth had been consummated at last!

It is a thrill to think upon our completion of the studies in this series, we will have traveled through the entire gospel of Luke together. But that does not excite me nearly as much as thinking that the gospel of Luke will have journeyed through our hearts. Or has it? Only time will tell . . . as Christ is allowed to live out His life through us.

Chuck Swindoll

# Putting Truth into Action

Knowledge apart from application falls short of God's desire for His children. He wants us to apply what we learn so that we will change and grow. This study guide was prepared with these goals in mind. As you go through the following pages, we hope your desire to discover biblical truth will grow as your understanding of God's Word increases and that you will be encouraged to apply what you've learned.

To assist you in your study, we've included a section called **Living Insights** at the end of each lesson. These exercises will challenge you to study further and to think of specific ways to put your discoveries into action.

On occasion a lesson is followed by a **Digging Deeper** section, which gives you additional information and resources to probe further into some issues raised in that lesson.

There are many ways to use this guide—in personal devotions, group studies, discussions with friends and family, and Sunday school classes. And, of course, it's an ideal study aid when you're listening to its corresponding *Insight for Living* radio series.

To benefit most from this study guide, we would encourage you to consider it a spiritual journal. That's why we've included space in the **Living Insights** for recording your thoughts and discoveries. We hope you'll return to those sections often for review and encouragement as you continue to grow in your walk with Christ.

Bryce Klabunde
Coauthor of Text
Author of Living Insights

# THE CONSUMMATION OF SOMETHING

# *Miraculous*

**Jesus' Trials and Triumph of Redemption**

A Study of Luke 16:19–24:53

# LUKE: A PHYSICIAN'S OPINION

**Writer:** Luke, a Gentile Christian physician (first mentioned in Acts 16:10)

**Date:** Around A.D. 60

**Style:** Scholarly, detailed, people-oriented

**Appeal:** Directly to Greeks, but universal

**Message:** Jesus is truly human

**Key Phrase:** "The Son of Man" (Luke 19:10)

**Interesting Facts:**

- This is the only gospel account specifically addressed to an individual: "most excellent Theophilus" (friend of God). William Barclay calls Luke 1:1–4, "well-nigh the best Greek in the New Testament."[1]
- Luke records the first hints of Christian hymnology (1:46–55, 68–79; 2:14, 29–32).
- More pictures have been painted by artists who derive their inspiration from Luke than any other New Testament book.
- Between chapters 9 and 19 there are over 30 sayings, parables, and incidents mentioned nowhere else in Scripture.

**The Son of Man . . .**

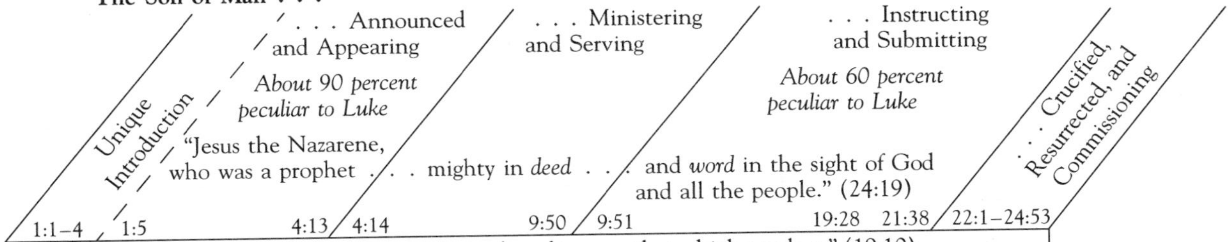

Unique Introduction (1:1–4)

. . . Announced and Appearing (1:5–4:13)
*About 90 percent peculiar to Luke*

. . . Ministering and Serving (4:14–9:50)

. . . Instructing and Submitting (9:51–21:38)
*About 60 percent peculiar to Luke*

. . . Crucified, Resurrected, and Commissioning (22:1–24:53)

"Jesus the Nazarene, who was a prophet . . . mighty in *deed* . . . and *word* in the sight of God and all the people." (24:19)

| | 1:1–4 / 1:5–4:13 | 4:14–9:50 | 9:51–19:28 | 19:28–21:38 | 22:1–24:53 |
|---|---|---|---|---|---|
| *Key Verse* | "For the Son of Man has come to seek and to save that which was lost." (19:10) | | | | |
| *Activity* | Coming | Seeking | | | Saving |
| *Location* | Bethlehem, Nazareth, and Judea | Galilee | Judea and Perea | Jerusalem | |
| *Time* | 30 years | $1\frac{1}{2}$ years | 6 mos. | 8 days | 50 days |



1. William Barclay, *The Gospel of Luke*, rev. ed., The Daily Study Bible Series (Philadelphia, Pa.: Westminster Press, 1975), p. 2.

Chapter 1

# THE SUBJECT EVERYBODY IGNORES

*Luke 16:19–31*

As we embark on this last leg of our journey through Luke's gospel, we find ourselves at an odd starting point: hell.

Who wants to talk about hell? Can't we discuss something more pleasant, like God's love for us or the riches of His salvation? Can't we just sort of bypass such a distasteful topic?

Not if we really want to comprehend the depth of His love and salvation.

"Think lightly of hell," said Charles Spurgeon,

> and you will think lightly of the cross. Think little of the sufferings of lost souls, and you will soon think little of the Savior who delivers you from them.[1]

Perhaps people don't take hell seriously because they view death as the ending, when it's really just the end of the beginning. To better grasp what's at stake in eternity, and to better appreciate Jesus' rescue of us, let's look at what the Bible reveals about death and what awaits us beyond the grave.

## A General Understanding of the Life Beyond

Death's bitter root reaches through time, all the way back to the Garden of Eden. Adam and Eve first planted its seed in the soil of humanity when they sinned against God and ate the forbidden fruit (see Gen. 2:16–17; 3:1–24). As a result of their disobedience, Paul writes,

> sin entered into the world, and death through sin,

1. C. H. Spurgeon, *Spurgeon at His Best*, comp. Tom Carter (Grand Rapids, Mich.: Baker Book House, 1988), p. 98.

and so death spread to all men, because all sinned. (Rom. 5:12)

From the moment we're born, our biological clocks start ticking away the time we have on earth. Death steadily, inevitably approaches, and its sheer mystery terrifies many of us. Thankfully, Scripture lifts some of the fog and shines a light into the afterlife, showing us what happens when we die.

As illustrated by the chart on the opposite page, when people die, only their bodies go into the grave. At a funeral it is merely the physical shell we see lying in the casket. The real person, the soul/spirit, has already departed to either a place of torment or a place of comfort, depending on the person's spiritual condition.

At Christ's ascension, many scholars believe that He brought the saints from "Abraham's bosom" to "the third heaven"[2]—to the realm where God lives (Eph. 4:8–10). Since then, believers' souls/spirits go immediately to be with Christ, awaiting the resurrection of their bodies when He returns. Later, at the final judgment, the bodies of unbelievers will be resurrected and joined with their souls/spirits to face an eternity in hell.

These facts give us a panorama of the afterlife. Jesus, though, wants to bring us up close, wants us to feel the burning breath of hell and taste the soothing relief of paradise. So He tells us a story in which He pulls back the ethereal curtain and escorts us into the realm of the dead.

## A Story Told of Two Who Died

Jesus has been teaching that no person can serve two masters; in particular, God and mammon (Luke 16:13). The money-loving Pharisees, however, have carved out a prosperous living under the guise of serving God, and they sneer at Jesus for His teaching (v. 14). Jesus' story emerges from this encounter and features three characters: the rich man, Lazarus, and Abraham.

### *A Study in Contrasts*

The first scene opens at the rich man's estate, where we find him enjoying a luxurious lifestyle. Just outside his gate lies Lazarus, the embodiment of poverty and pain.

2. The first heaven is the sky and the second is space.

# When People Die . . . What Happens?

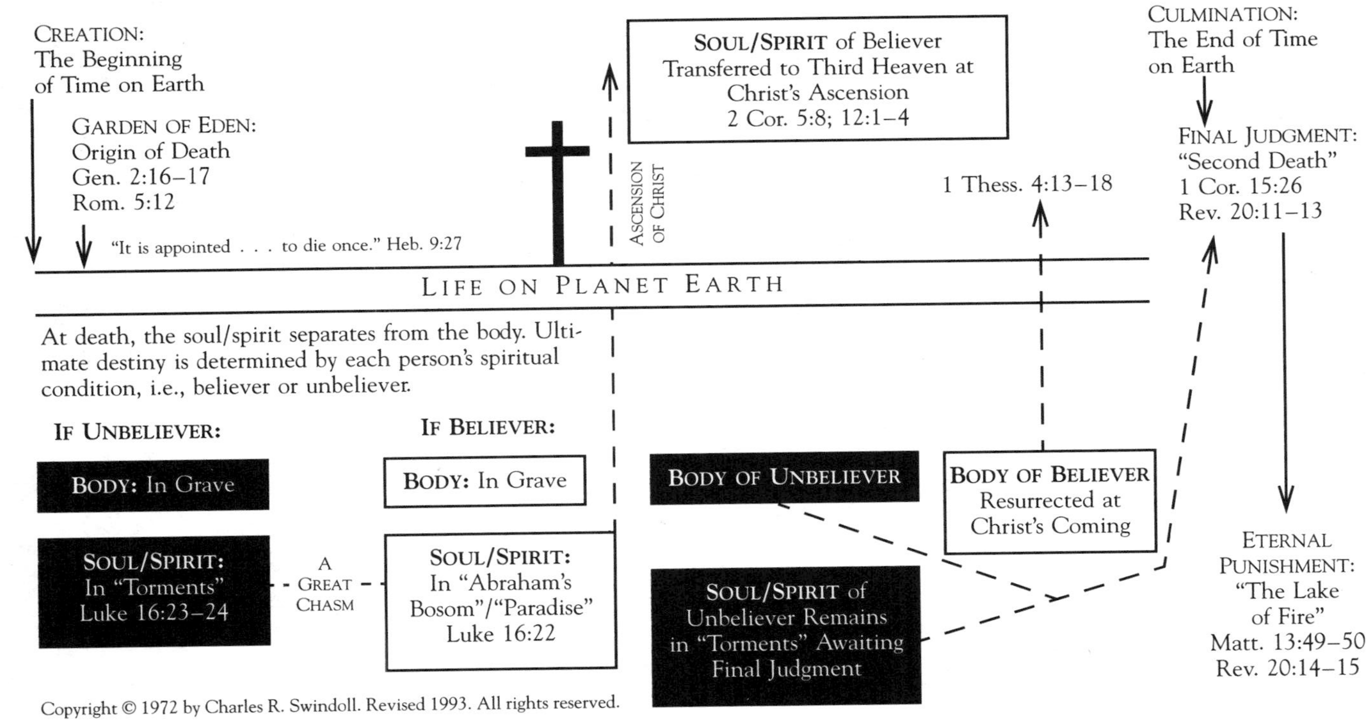

Creation:
The Beginning
of Time on Earth
Garden of Eden:
Origin of Death
Gen. 2:16–17
Rom. 5:12
"It is appointed . . . to die once." Heb. 9:27
Soul/Spirit of Believer
Transferred to Third Heaven at
Christ's Ascension
2 Cor. 5:8; 12:1–4
Ascension of Christ
1 Thess. 4:13–18
Culmination:
The End of Time
on Earth
Final Judgment:
"Second Death"
1 Cor. 15:26
Rev. 20:11–13
Life on Planet Earth
At death, the soul/spirit separates from the body. Ultimate destiny is determined by each person's spiritual condition, i.e., believer or unbeliever.
If Unbeliever:
Body: In Grave
Soul/Spirit:
In "Torments"
Luke 16:23–24
A Great Chasm
If Believer:
Body: In Grave
Soul/Spirit:
In "Abraham's
Bosom"/"Paradise"
Luke 16:22
Body of Unbeliever
Body of Believer
Resurrected at
Christ's Coming
Soul/Spirit of
Unbeliever Remains
in "Torments" Awaiting
Final Judgment
Eternal
Punishment:
"The Lake
of Fire"
Matt. 13:49–50
Rev. 20:14–15

> "Now there was a certain rich man, and he habitually dressed in purple and fine linen, gaily living in splendor every day. And a certain poor man named Lazarus was laid at his gate, covered with sores, and longing to be fed with the crumbs which were falling from the rich man's table; besides, even the dogs were coming and licking his sores." (vv. 16:19–21)

The rich man, pampered and indulged, lived on a mountain peak of wealth and privilege. Lazarus, however, lived in the valley of the shadow of death. The rich man habitually dressed in the most expensive garments; Lazarus was clothed in open sores. The rich man savored the good life *every day*; Lazarus hungered for the dog's scraps while the dogs fed on his wounds. The rich man averted his eyes from the pitiful beggar slumped by his front gate. But Lazarus looked to the rich man for mercy and help.

No help, however, was ever to come.

> "Now it came about that the poor man died and he was carried away by the angels to Abraham's bosom; and the rich man also died and was buried." (v. 22)

When Lazarus died, his body was probably carted away to the city dump and burned with the trash. The rich man, no doubt, had an elaborate, well-attended funeral and was buried in a lavish tomb. Yet, as the two men's souls passed through death's portal, an amazing reversal occurred. Angelic pallbearers bore Lazarus' soul to Paradise, while the rich man's soul was unceremoniously pitched into the fires of hell.[3]

### An Analysis of Future Torment

> "And in Hades he lifted up his eyes, being in torment, and saw Abraham far away, and Lazarus in his bosom. And he cried out and said, 'Father Abraham, have mercy on me, and send Lazarus, that he may dip the tip of his finger in water and cool off my

3. Did God condemn the rich man to this horrible fate because he was wealthy? Did Lazarus receive bliss because he was poor? No, Scripture says that where we place our faith determines our destinies (John 3:36). The rich man trusted the things of this world and cared nothing for the things of God's kingdom. Lazarus' faith in God is revealed in his name, which "is the Latinized form of Eleazar and means *God is my help*." William Barclay, *The Gospel of Luke*, rev. ed., The Daily Study Bible Series (Philadelphia, Pa.: Westminster Press, 1975), p. 214.

> tongue; for I am in agony in this flame.' But Abraham said, 'Child, remember that during your life you received your good things, and likewise Lazarus bad things; but now he is being comforted here, and you are in agony. And besides all this, between us and you there is a great chasm fixed, in order that those who wish to come over from here to you may not be able, and that none may cross over from there to us.'" (vv. 23–26)

In life, the rich man wore silk and indulged his palate with the finest wines; now flames sear his skin, and he aches for just a drop of water to cool his swollen tongue.

Through the lens of this story, Jesus gives us a frightening glimpse into hell. Mercifully, it's only a brief look, but it is powerful enough to blow apart four common rationalizations that discount the severity of hell.

1. "*Hell will be a relief compared to the suffering we endure on earth.*" While Lazarus did suffer terribly, the rich man was now enduring "torment" and "agony" far beyond that of the poor beggar during life (vv. 23–24). Puritan preacher Thomas Hooker explains hell's anguish this way:

> Conceive thus much, if all the diseases in the world did seize on one man, and if all torments that all the tyrants in the world could devise, were cast upon him; and if all the creatures in heaven and earth did conspire the destruction of this man; and if all the devils in hell did labor to inflict punishments upon him, you would think this man to be in a miserable condition. And yet all this is but a beam of God's indignation. If the beams of God's indignation be so hot, what is the full sum of his wrath, when it shall seize upon the soul of a sinful creature in full measure?[4]

2. "*All this stuff about hell is based on imaginative fears; when we die, we will feel and know nothing.*" Jesus' story, however, shows the opposite: the rich man sees (v. 23), feels (v. 24), talks with Abraham (vv. 24–31), and tastes (v. 24). He even remembers the "good things" he received on earth and how he selfishly hoarded them (v. 25).

4. Thomas Hooker, as quoted by Jon E. Braun, in *Whatever Happened to Hell?* (Nashville, Tenn.: Thomas Nelson Publishers, 1979), pp. 83–84.

3. *"Hell won't be so bad; I'll be there with all my buddies!"* We don't see the rich man resting in the companionship of his friends like Lazarus rests in the bosom of Abraham. He suffers alone. No one puts an arm around him or dampens his feverish brow. He is utterly abandoned—forever within sight, but never within reach, of Paradise.

4. *"After I'm in hell for awhile, somebody will pray me out."* But remember Abraham's words? "Between us and you there is a great chasm fixed . . . none may cross over" (v. 26). No bridge exists to the other side. There is no purgatory, no reincarnation, no chance for relief. Dante's inscription over the gates of hell in his epic poem "The Inferno" states the stark reality:

> I am the way into the city of woe.
> I am the way to a forsaken people.
> I am the way into eternal sorrow. . . .
>
> Only those elements time cannot wear
> Were made before me, and beyond time I stand.
> Abandon all hope ye who enter here.[5]

### *A Plea for Those Still Living*

Grasping the permanence of his doom, the rich man pictures his five brothers, who will suffer similar fates unless they turn their hearts toward the Lord. For the first time in his entire self-absorbed life, he thinks of others:

> "And he said, 'Then I beg you, Father, that you send him to my father's house—for I have five brothers—that he may warn them, lest they also come to this place of torment.' But Abraham said, 'They have Moses and the Prophets; let them hear them.' But he said, 'No, Father Abraham, but if someone goes to them from the dead, they will repent!'" (vv. 16:27–30)

This is the real tragedy. All along, the rich man knew that salvation depended on repentance. He had heard the message of Moses and the Prophets. Yet he chose not to turn from the darkness while he had the chance. Now he is afraid his brothers will ignore

5. Dante Alighieri, "The Inferno," in *The Divine Comedy*, trans. John Ciardi (New York, N.Y.: W. W. Norton and Co., 1970), p. 13.

Scripture too, so he hopes a ghost might frighten them into the light. But, shaking his head, Abraham responds,

> "'If they do not listen to Moses and the Prophets, neither will they be persuaded if someone rises from the dead.'" (v. 31b)

## A Summary of Lessons Learned

With that thought, Jesus closes the curtain to the afterlife and ushers us back into the present. But we do not return empty-handed, for we carry with us three valuable lessons.

First, *God's written Word is the most important evidence a person can examine*. God's Word is "living and active and sharper than any two-edged sword" (Heb. 4:12a). Our Bibles, with their gilt-edged pages, may not look like swords to us. We'd rather wield the flaming blades of miracles and visions. But God's Word alone can pierce "as far as the division of soul and spirit" and "judge the thoughts and intentions of the heart" (v. 12b). It can change lives.

Second, *God's written Word is the most compelling information to prepare us for life after death*. People may prepare for death by writing wills or increasing their life insurance, but that won't help them after death. Only God's Word can show us how to repent and live for Christ so we're ready to enter His presence with joy.

Third, *the person who ignores the Word of God in life will not be ignored by the God of the Word in eternity*. Jesus' story flashes a somber warning: death is sure, hell is real, God will judge. Such a message refuses to leave us neutral toward the lost souls of our world. May we see them in the light of their eternal destiny. May we take the subject of hell as seriously as Jesus did. And may we always remember what drove Him to the Cross.

## *Living Insights* STUDY ONE

Usually, we hide the subject of hell in the basement of our theology, somewhere in a cobwebbed corner, tucked behind a croquet set and a box of bowling trophies. Once in a while, we dust it off and bring it upstairs, but it doesn't seem to fit well with the theologies we have on display: sovereignty, worship, hope, the goodness of God.

Still, we set it on a shelf, thinking we'll get used to it. The longer it sits there, though, the more it disturbs us. We begin to wonder:

- How can a loving God send people to hell?
- What about those who have never heard the gospel?
- Is a person's deathbed repentance valid?
- What about babies who die?

How would you answer these questions? Let's dig into the Scriptures and see if we can formulate some responses. A note of caution though: God's Word is His message to us, but it is not the totality of who God is. He is a big God—too big to be packaged in neat little answers. He is a God of mystery, and sometimes we have to accept and live with not knowing.

1. The God who "sends people to hell" is also the One who sacrificed His own Son to provide a way out. What do John 3:16–17, Romans 5:6–11, 1 Timothy 2:1–6, and 2 Peter 3:9 tell you about God's character and will?

   ______________________________________________

   ______________________________________________

   ______________________________________________

   Perhaps the real issue is not why God "sends" people to hell but why people *choose* hell. What insights does John 3:18–21 give you?

   ______________________________________________

   ______________________________________________

   ______________________________________________

2. The next question is harder: What about those who have never heard the gospel? In pondering this issue, we need to first remember God's character—see Psalms 86:15, 119:137, and Isaiah 30:18. Next, consider God's response to a seeker in Acts 10:1–8. Finally, pray through Romans 1:19–20 and 2:11–16. What conclusions do you come to? (Remember, it's OK if your response is very much like Paul's in Romans 11:33–36.)

   ______________________________________________

3. Jesus Himself answers the deathbed repentance question. See Luke 23:39–43 and also Matthew 20:1–16.
4. Parents reeling at the loss of a baby don't need to also struggle with fear for their little one's eternal destiny. Another grieving parent, David, had comfort in the absolute knowledge that he would spend eternity with his infant. See 2 Samuel 12:19–23.[6]

Ignoring the tough subject of hell may be our instinctual reaction to a frightening topic. But as we have seen through pondering these questions, only when we turn fully to look at it can we see how dazzlingly our salvation shines against hell's black backdrop.

## *Living Insights* STUDY TWO

Why would Jesus speak about hell at this point in His ministry? To pique His listeners' interest? To scare up a bigger following? Not at all.

If we look at the overall context of Luke 16, we'll see that the story of the rich man and Lazarus, of heaven and hell, is the graphic climax to which Jesus has been building. His theme? *We must spend our lives—and our property and possessions—with eternity in view* (vv. 9–13). Not because we work our way into heaven, but because our deeds are the outworking of our hearts. Commentator Michael Wilcock explains:

> Our destiny in that world depends on what we do with the "here and now." [This story] is a challenge to the far-sighted use of the things of this world, the things we shall not be able to take with us, but which nonetheless constitute the raw material out of which our inner character is built.[7]

6. For further study, we recommend the following resources: Robert A. Morey's *Death and the Afterlife* (Minneapolis, Minn.: Bethany House Publishers, 1984); and Charles R. Swindoll's *Growing Deep in the Christian Life* (Portland, Oreg.: Multnomah Press, 1986), pp. 322–26.

7. Michael Wilcock, *The Message of Luke*, The Bible Speaks Today Series (Downers Grove, Ill.: InterVarsity Press, 1979), p. 162.

Those in Jesus' audience who most needed but least heeded such a forceful lesson were the money-loving Pharisees (vv. 14–15). As author Ken Gire noted, "They are the rich men living in luxury, while the Lazaruses of this world are dying just outside their gates."[8]

Unlike the Pharisees, we may have escaped hell's fires by trusting Christ for our salvation. Yet we can still harbor Pharisaic attitudes toward those in need. Let's take some time now to examine our hearts before the Lord.

Who is the Lazarus just outside your gate, who is dying physically, emotionally, or spiritually?

---

How have you responded to this person—with compassionate care, indifference, blame, contempt?

---

---

Are you like the rich man? Then please, earnestly consider the penetrating words of William Barclay:

> The sin of Dives [the rich man] was that he never noticed Lazarus, that he accepted him as part of the landscape and simply thought it perfectly natural and inevitable that Lazarus should lie in pain and hunger while he wallowed in luxury. . . . The sin of Dives was that he could look on the world's suffering and need and feel no answering sword of grief and pity pierce his heart; he looked at a fellow man, hungry and in pain, and did nothing about it.[9]

How we treat the "least of these" really does matter to Jesus (see Matt. 25:31–46). The rich man learned too late. Will we?

8. Ken Gire, *Instructive Moments with the Savior* (Grand Rapids, Mich.: Zondervan Publishing House, 1992), p. 75.

9. Barclay, *The Gospel of Luke*, p. 214.

Chapter 2

# How Not to Be a Stumbling Block

*Luke 17:1–19*

"When I was a lad," the old man confessed to loved ones gathered during his last hours, "I often played on a wide common. Near its centre two roads met and crossed, and, standing at the crossroads, was an old rickety sign post." A troubled frown clouded his face. "I remember one day twisting it round in its socket, thus altering the arms and making them point in the wrong direction; and I've been wondering ever since how many travellers I sent on the wrong road."[1]

Whether along a country road or the path of life, leading people astray exacts a heavy toll on both the innocent and the guilty. Scripture says that each of us has the potential of causing others to go wrong. Each of us, if we're not careful, can become a stumbling block.

## How We Can Become Stumbling Blocks

We can hinder people from following Christ in at least three ways. First, *by what we say*. James warns us,

> Let not many of you become teachers, my brethren, knowing that as such we shall incur a stricter judgment. For we all stumble in many ways. If anyone does not stumble in what he says, he is a perfect man, able to bridle the whole body as well. (James 3:1–2)

Since we all know that no one but Christ is perfect, we also know we're bound to stumble in what we say. James singles out those of us who instruct or counsel others because these positions carry more influence. By inaccurately or carelessly teaching God's truth, we can trip up many people who genuinely yearn to follow Christ.

Second, we can become stumbling blocks *by the way we live*. Paul, for example, cautions us not to flaunt our freedom in Christ:

> Take care lest this liberty of yours somehow become

1. William Barclay, *The Gospel of Luke*, rev. ed., The Daily Study Bible Series (Philadelphia, Pa.: Westminster Press, 1975), p. 216.

> a stumbling block to the weak. (1 Cor. 8:9)

Without love's restraint, we can disfigure grace with arrogance and disregard for others. Our actions can confuse weaker Christians, leading them to violate their consciences and return to their former sins.

Third, we can become stumbling blocks *by the way we think*. Our judgmental attitudes can feel like quicksand to others, smothering their joy and excitement in Christ. "Therefore," Paul exhorts us,

> let us not judge one another anymore, but rather determine this—not to put an obstacle or a stumbling block in a brother's way. (Rom. 14:13)

God's message couldn't be clearer: Don't be a stumbling block! In fact, over in Luke 17, Jesus even thunders a "woe" to those who make hazardous the paths of others (v. 1; compare 11:42–52). Let's turn to His words now, which will help us clear, rather than obstruct, the way for fellow travelers trying to follow Him.

## What It Means to Be a Stumbling Block

With a telling glance at the Pharisees, Jesus warns His disciples:

> "It is inevitable that stumbling blocks should come, but woe to him through whom they come!" (17:1)

The Greek word translated *stumbling blocks* is *skandalon*, which means "the bait-stick of a trap, that which triggers off trouble."[2] Jesus is saying that people are bound to wander into temptation and feel sin's consequences, like steel jaws, snap shut on their lives. But woe to the one who sets the trap!

Woe to the adult who leads the innocent child into sin.
Woe to the preacher who deceives the gullible believer.
Woe to the counselor who seduces the emotionally fragile client.
Woe to the legalistic Pharisee who misrepresents God.

Concerning those who bring harm, Jesus says,

> "It would be better for him if a millstone were hung around his neck and he were thrown into the sea, than that he should cause one of these little ones to stumble." (v. 2)

2. Leon Morris, *The Gospel according to St. Luke*, The Tyndale New Testament Commentaries Series (Grand Rapids, Mich.: William B. Eerdmans Publishing Co., 1974), p. 255. We get our English word *scandal* from this root.

Have you ever seen a millstone? It's a large circular stone that rests flat on top of another. An axle is fitted through it, and an ox pulls it in a circle to pulverize raw grain into fine powder. Since it is much too heavy to lift, the stone would be rolled into the sea, and down you'd go with it.

Jesus uses this frightful image to make a vivid point: this horrid death would be a better end than the judgment for leading someone away from God.

So, "Be on your guard!" Jesus cautions His disciples (v. 3a). Don't just cluck your tongue at the Pharisees; take heed to yourselves too (compare Gal. 6:1). Jesus next gives some preventive counsel so we can learn how to avoid becoming a stumbling block.

## How to Keep from Becoming a Stumbling Block

Jesus' message in these verses seems to jump from point to point, like a rock skipping across water. Yet, if we look closely, however, great depth and power lie beneath the surface of each subject.

### *Quickly, Completely, and Repeatedly Forgive*

> "If your brother sins, rebuke him; and if he repents, forgive him. And if he sins against you seven times a day, and returns to you seven times, saying, 'I repent,' forgive him." (Luke 17:3b–4)

The "rebuke" part comes more naturally to us than the "forgive" part, doesn't it? Like the Pharisees, we feel a sense of satisfaction in hooking an offender with a well-cast rebuke and reeling the rascal in. The hard part is letting the sinner go when he or she repents. And not just once, but again and again.

Forgiving is not so much excusing the offender's guilt as releasing the person in God's grace and freeing ourselves to live without pain. It's as much for our benefit as the other person's. For by unhooking the offender, we unhook ourselves from the bitterness and anger that can sour our lives and turn us into stumbling blocks to the people around us. Our forgiveness gives people a sweet taste of Christ's forgiveness, a taste that will draw them to Him rather than point them away.

### *Encourage Great Faith*

Forgive seven times in a single day? That's not humanly possible, which the disciples pick up on right away:

> And the apostles said to the Lord, "Increase our faith!" (v. 5)

Jesus, however, reveals that the amount of faith is not the issue.

> And the Lord said, "If you had faith like a mustard seed, you would say to this mulberry tree, 'Be uprooted and be planted in the sea'; and it would obey you." (v. 6)

Even a tiny amount of faith in God can accomplish the impossible. Commentator Leon Morris pinpoints the real issue: "It is not so much great faith in God that is required as faith in a great God."[3]

There's not an ounce of uncertainty in Jesus' mind that His disciples will be able to follow His commands, because they have the power of God on their side. And with Him, anything is possible (see 18:27)!

May it never be said that we were the death of someone else's dream—that we crushed their "mustard-seed" faith under the fearsome size of the "mulberry tree." When "What ifs" and "Be carefuls" and "Watch outs" start pouring out of our mouths, we become stumbling blocks. Jesus was a "Go for it!" kind of person. Let's be "Go for it!" people too.

### *Model True Servanthood*

Faith and obedience lead Jesus to another subject: servanthood.

> "But which of you, having a slave plowing or tending sheep, will say to him when he has come in from the field, 'Come immediately and sit down to eat'? But will he not say to him, 'Prepare something for me to eat, and properly clothe yourself and serve me until I have eaten and drunk; and afterward you will eat and drink'? He does not thank the slave because he did the things which were commanded, does he? So you too, when you do all the things which are commanded you, say, 'We are unworthy slaves; we have done only that which we ought to have done.'" (17:7–10)

Let's put Jesus' illustration in military terms to better understand

3. Morris, *The Gospel according to St. Luke*, p. 256.

it. Suppose a drill sergeant commands a private, "Make your bunk, and shine your shoes," and the private immediately obeys. Does the sergeant now owe the private a thank-you and a favor? Not in any army we've heard of! The private was simply fulfilling his duty.

In a similar way, true servants of Christ should not expect favors from God when they do what they're supposed to do. We can never say, "Lord, I had a loving attitude today, so You owe me three blessings and an answered prayer." God does not owe us gratitude; we owe Him! He is not our servant; we are His servants. Pharisaical pride in ourselves and our accomplishments will definitely send others sprawling, but the right perspective of humility will gently aid others on their way.

### *Take Time to Say "Thank You"*

Too often, while we're waiting for God to thank us, we forget to thank Him.

> And it came about while He was on the way to Jerusalem, that He was passing between Samaria and Galilee. And as He entered a certain village, ten leprous men who stood at a distance met Him; and they raised their voices, saying, "Jesus, Master, have mercy on us!" (vv. 11–13)

Jewish law swept lepers into isolated colonies and required them to tear their clothes, bare their heads, and, whenever anyone ventured too close, cry out in humiliation, "Unclean! Unclean!" (see Lev. 13:45–46).

So they stand at a distance from Jesus—ten tattered refugees in a war with death. Some of their features have been eaten away; some of their fingers and toes as well. Even hands and feet. Their one hope is Jesus, whose mercy does not let them down.

> And when He saw them, He said to them, "Go and show yourselves to the priests." And it came about that as they were going, they were cleansed. Now one of them, when he saw that he had been healed, turned back, glorifying God with a loud voice, and he fell on his face at His feet, giving thanks to Him. And he was a Samaritan. And Jesus answered and said, "Were there not ten cleansed? But the nine—where are they? Was no one found who turned back

to give glory to God, except this foreigner?" And He said to him, "Rise, and go your way; your faith has made you well." (Luke 17:14–19)

Ten are healed. Nine leave and never come back; one returns to offer thanks—a Samaritan. A heretic to the Jews, he is the only one who exhibits genuine faith. So Jesus blesses him, giving him a clean heart to match his fresh, new skin.

The story compels us to think of the people who have played the role of Christ in our lives. Our parents, who gave us life and nurtured us through difficult years. Our friends, who offered us hope and encouragement. A physician. A counselor. A pastor. A teacher. Have we neglected to say thank you? Has our taking them for granted become a stumbling block to them?

## Two Things worth Remembering

Few of us wake up in the morning and say to ourselves, "Today, I'm going to trip someone and make them fall." Most of the time, it happens unintentionally. That's why we need to keep in mind these two points.

First, *it's usually not the big things that cause others to stumble, but the little things*. Jokes can be taken the wrong way. Expressions can be misunderstood. We can thoughtlessly offend someone and not even realize it. That's why it's important for us to pay attention to the small things.

Second, *it's usually not what we do that offends people, it's what we don't do*. We never actually forgive someone. We hold back an encouraging word. We don't raise our hand to serve. We forget to say thank you. In each of these ways, we can be a stumbling block to someone. But the good news is, we don't have to remain that way. Stone by stone, we can tear down the barrier we've erected. And we can begin with the simple but powerful words, "I'm sorry."

## *Living Insights* STUDY ONE

Dressed in teddy bear overalls, the wobbly toddler crouches on all fours, trying to shift his weight to his pudgy legs. With the concentration of an Olympic weight lifter, he steadies himself and slowly rises to his full two-and-a-half feet height. The audience cheers—mom, dad, a couple of aunts, and grandma. "C'mon, honey," mom coaxes. His hands held aloft for balance, the little fellow leans forward and takes one jerky step. Then two. Three. Four. He's walking!

Watching a toddler learn to walk is one of the greatest delights of parenting—a joy the Lord must feel when He sees His children take their first spiritual steps. The heavens must reverberate with the Father's cheering when a new Christian mouths his first prayer or discovers her first biblical insight.

Imagine, then, His anger when someone sticks out a foot and trips up His precious child. Or when, because of gossip or judgmental criticism or false teaching, one of His little ones falls into confusion and sin.

None of us would think of tripping a toddler; neither would we intentionally become a stumbling block to one of God's children. Yet it happens, sometimes without our realizing it.

In the lesson, we talked about four ways we can avoid becoming stumbling blocks: forgiving, encouraging, humbly serving, thanking. Take some time to review your relationships. Have the opposites of Jesus' counsel—bitterness, neglect, pride, or ingratitude—seeped into any of them and caused someone to slip?

________________________________________

________________________________________

________________________________________

________________________________________

What can you do to put that child of God back on his or her feet again? Is there an idea from 1 Corinthians 13:4–7 you can use?

________________________________________

________________________________________

________________________________________

________________________________________

Little ones are bound to stumble. But if we learn to see God's children as He sees them and love as He loves, we can be the Father's hands to catch them when they fall.

## *Living Insights*



Gratitude does not grow well in the crusty soil of pride. For a thankful spirit to blossom, we must cultivate humility in our hearts. And to do that, we must see ourselves accurately.

Luke holds before us as a mirror the story of the ten lepers. We are the lepers, standing at a distance, wearing the rags of our works. We try to conceal the disease of sin that is slowly consuming our flesh, but Christ sees us as we are. Unclean. Ostracized. Dying.

Without Christ, what will happen to us in our state of sin (see Rom. 2:5–9; 2 Thess. 1:8–9)?

________________________________________

________________________________________

Dangling over the edge of an abyss, we cry out to Him, "Jesus, Master, have mercy on us!" He does not owe us anything. We have done nothing to deserve His favor (see 2 Tim. 1:8–9). Only by His mercy will He toss us a line and pull us out of death's black hole.

Prayerfully consider Psalm 51:1–2. What divine attributes motivate God's mercy?

________________________________________

________________________________________

He calls to us, "Go and show yourselves to the priests." It seems a bit crazy, but we grab hold of His words and hurry away. As we obey in faith, our sores begin to dry up. The redness fades. The scabs fall off to reveal clean, fresh skin. Our sins have been washed away, and we are healed!

According to Colossians 1:13–14 and 2:13, what has Christ done for us?

________________________________________

________________________________________

Does putting yourself inside the story of the ten lepers stir a spirit of thanksgiving in your heart? Take a moment to read Psalm 103:1–5, then use the following space to remember His benefits in your life and, like the one returning leper, fall before Jesus' feet and thank Him.

Chapter 3

# Knowing Where You Are . . . Knowing Where You're Going

*Luke 17:20–37*

The old Irishman, a rosy-cheeked man in a tweed jacket and tam-o'-shanter, placed his hands on Carson's shoulders. Looking into his eyes, he said soberly, "Don't forget to be lookin' behind ya to make sure you're goin' in the right direction."

Carson laughed to himself, convinced that this was some sort of Irish joke. OK, he was on to them now—he'd get himself and his father past Dublin and south to Waterford by his own wits. Thanking the man, Carson joined his father in the car and drove off . . . and promptly got lost. They arrived at their relative's house hours late.

Warming themselves by the peat fire, they recounted the story, ". . . and then the man said, 'Don't forget to be lookin' behind ya to make sure you're goin' in the right direction,'" and burst into laughter. However, no one else laughed.

His sister-in-law's mother looked at Carson and said, "Well, did ya?"

"What do you mean, 'Did ya?'"

"Did ya look behind ya?"

Carson stared at her blankly.

She explained, "When they were puttin' up the highway signs, they started in the south and worked toward Dublin, but they ran out of money. Sure an' the only way you can tell that you're on the right highway is to look behind ya."[1]

"Look behind ya." That's good advice, whether we're traveling the highways of Ireland or the highways of life. Our clearest view of what lies ahead, paradoxically, is often through hindsight's 20/20 vision.

## Three Benefits Gleaned from Hindsight

A good look in the rearview mirror benefits us in at least three ways.

1. Adapted from a story told by Carson Pue, executive director of Insight for Living Ministries (British Columbia, Canada), at an Insight for Living chapel service, September 14, 1994.

1. *Looking back forces us to be realistic.* Knowing where we've been tethers our dreams to reality so we can plan wisely for the future.

2. *Looking back encourages us when we see how God has worked.* When we recall where we were a year ago, how grateful we can be for how far He has brought us today.

3. *Looking back humbles us when we recall our shortcomings, mistakes, and failures.* Like markers along the road, our mistakes reveal the direction we've been heading. If we're teachable and want to grow from them, though, we get another chance to change course.

As Jesus prepares us for the future in Luke 17, let's not "forget to be lookin' behind" us as well. As we consider how we've lived, His words can help us evaluate where we are and, if need be, set a new direction.

## Five Pieces of Advice Inferred from Jesus' Words

From Jesus' exchange first with the Pharisees and then with His disciples, we can identify five signposts that will help us know we're on the right road.

### *God Is in Your Midst*

When we last saw Jesus, He had miraculously and mercifully healed ten lepers, which makes the Pharisees' question in the next verse all the more ironic. "When is the kingdom of God coming?" they want to know (see Luke 17:20a). So Jesus points out the obvious:

> "The kingdom of God is not coming with signs to be observed; nor will they say, 'Look, here it is!' or, 'There it is!' For behold, *the kingdom of God is in your midst*." (vv. 20b–21, emphasis added)

"It's standing right in front of you!" Jesus says. The presence and power of God were in Christ. The kingdom was in their here and now, not just in the lightning streaks of a distant future. Yet the Pharisees wanted no part of Jesus, so they disdainfully brushed aside the very thing they supposedly sought (see 11:14–15).[2]

Like the Pharisees, we sometimes search the skies for signs of

2. The phrase *in your midst* can mean "within you." Some use this translation to prove that the kingdom of God is spiritual only. However, it is unlikely that Jesus would tell the Pharisees the kindgom of God was within them.

God while overlooking His footprints in the sand of our lives. Take the past year of your life, for example. How has God provided for you, protected you, guided you, matured you? Perhaps it wasn't anything spectacular, but the point is: *Though it may not have been obvious or exciting, God's power has continued to be in your midst.* What an encouraging reminder! And something to be grateful for too (compare 17:15–16).

### *God's Plan Is Unfolding*

How can Jesus tell the Pharisees about His second coming when they don't even recognize His first coming? "The disciples, on the other hand," writes commentator Michael Wilcock,

> had the discernment to see both comings. They had accepted, and indeed been sent themselves to preach, the present reality of the kingdom (9:2, 10:9), so Jesus can now go on to tell them something about "the days of the Son of man" (17:26).[3]

So, turning to His disciples, Jesus says,

> "The days shall come when you will long to see one of the days of the Son of Man, and you will not see it. And they will say to you, 'Look there! Look here!' Do not go away, and do not run after them. For just as the lightning, when it flashes out of one part of the sky, shines to the other part of the sky, so will the Son of Man be in His day." (vv. 22–24)

Ever the loving teacher, Jesus continues to prepare His disciples for the long days of waiting for His return after He leaves the earth. He knows the disciples' hearts will yearn for Him and the coming of His kingdom (v. 22). Yet He also knows that too desperate a longing will make them vulnerable to being misled (v. 23). So He assures them that their patience will be gloriously rewarded by His coming, which will be unmistakable by its speed and worldwide scope (v. 24).

Before the disciples get too wrapped up in coming glory, however, Jesus reminds them that the Cross must come first.

3. Michael Wilcock, *The Message of Luke*, The Bible Speaks Today Series (Downers Grove, Ill.: InterVarsity Press, 1979), p. 163.

"But first He must suffer many things and be rejected by this generation." (v. 25)

How can we apply all this to our lives today? In the midst of hardship, depression, or pain, we often hear people telling us to "Look there!" or "Look here!" for answers apart from God. Their advice makes us feel like we're wasting our time waiting on the Lord. After a while, we start to wonder if they're right.

At times like these, remember what Jesus showed His disciples: He will come again in power and in glory (v. 24). Our principle, then, for everyday affairs is this: *Although waiting for a breakthrough may seem like wasted effort, God's plan is unfolding.* We may not understand how God is shaping our lives, but we can be sure that no one will "ward off His hand" from accomplishing His will for us (Dan. 4:35; see also Phil. 1:6; Heb. 12:2a).

### *God's Time Clock Is Ticking*

"Stay faithful while you're waiting for my return," Jesus seems to be saying. Unfortunately, though, many won't be ready when judgment suddenly does come.

> "And just as it happened in the days of Noah, so it shall be also in the days of the Son of Man: they were eating, they were drinking, they were marrying, they were being given in marriage, until the day that Noah entered the ark, and the flood came and destroyed them all. It was the same as happened in the days of Lot: they were eating, they were drinking, they were buying, they were selling, they were planting, they were building; but on the day that Lot went out from Sodom it rained fire and brimstone from heaven and destroyed them all. It will be just the same on the day that the Son of Man is revealed." (Luke 17:26–30)

Years later, Peter would echo His Lord's words:

> In the last days mockers will come with their mocking, following after their own lusts, and saying, "Where is the promise of His coming? For ever since the fathers fell asleep, all continues just as it was from the beginning of creation." (2 Pet. 3:3–4)

Yet all hasn't continued just the same. The world was once destroyed with a flood, and it will be again with fire (vv. 5–7). Just because God's judgment hasn't come doesn't mean it's a myth. God's timing is simply different than ours:

> With the Lord one day is as a thousand years, and a thousand years as one day. The Lord is not slow about His promise, as some count slowness, but is patient toward you, not wishing for any to perish but for all to come to repentance. (vv. 8b–9)

Peter learned well from Christ's words, and so can we. Our principle to remember? *The humdrum routine of living does not mean promises are forgotten or deadlines canceled. God's time clock is still ticking.* And Jesus doesn't want us caught unaware.

### *God Takes No Pleasure in Our Clinging*

Jesus' next piece of counsel reflects a theme He has woven throughout His ministry: our life does not consist of our possessions (see Luke 12:15–34).

> "On that day, let not the one who is on the housetop and whose goods are in the house go down to take them away; and likewise let not the one who is in the field turn back. Remember Lot's wife. Whoever seeks to keep his life shall lose it, and whoever loses his life shall preserve it." (17:31–33)

Lot's wife, remember, thought her life was made up of her house, her community standing, her standard of living. She mistook these externals for the real life—spiritual life. By looking back toward her burning home in Sodom, she was clinging to her way of life, and she ultimately lost all (see Gen. 19:24–26).

Jesus is telling His disciples to instead keep their hearts clear, keep their riches with God. "Don't lose your life over such transitory, perishable things," He urges.

The principle to remember is this: *Holding everything loosely is still the best option worth pursuing, because God takes no pleasure in our clinging.* If the Lord's Judgment-Day demolition crew appeared at your door one morning, could you leave everything behind without looking back? If not, maybe your grip on things is too tight—or maybe things have too tight a grip on you.

### *God's Judgments Are Individual Judgments*

Building on His distinction between those who have kept their lives for themselves and those who have lost their lives for His sake, Jesus tells His disciples what will happen to both groups.

> "I tell you, on that night there will be two men in one bed; one will be taken, and the other will be left. There will be two women grinding at the same place; one will be taken, and the other will be left. Two men will be in the field; one will be taken and the other will be left." And answering they said to Him, "Where, Lord?" And He said to them, "Where the body is, there also will the vultures be gathered." (Luke 17:34–37)

Those whose life is with God, Jesus says, will be taken away, receiving blessing and vindication. Unbelievers, however, who have lived apart from God, will be left behind to endure His judgment, which will descend on them like vultures on a dead body.

As you review your life, what road of faith do the signs say you've been traveling? Perhaps you've assumed you were saved because you hung around with Christians, attended Christian events, and tried to live a Christian life. However, you can't network your way into heaven. Remember: *Spending time with Christians is no guarantee of your own salvation; God's judgments are individual judgments*. He examines one person, one heart, one life at a time.

## Two Things We Can Do about It

Having listened to Jesus' counsel and also looked "behind ya," can you tell whether you're on the right highway? Two more signs can help you find out. First, *look deep within your own life*. It's tempting to blame others for our problems. But God holds us, not our neighbors or our families, responsible for our choices. Only we can tell whether we're traveling on the right road and whether we're ready for Christ's return.

Second, *look high above your own circumstances*. Does your journey seem hard? Are you wondering if it's worth it all? Get a fresh view of Christ and His love for you. Weigh what has you anxious and upset on the scale of eternity. And set your eyes on the destination—your glorious home with Him.

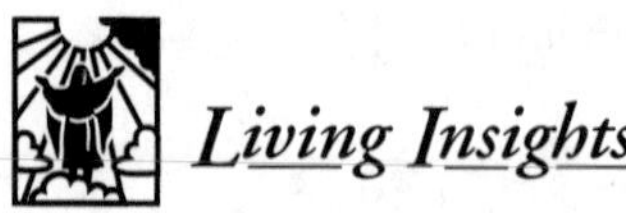

## *Living Insights*

STUDY ONE

> "For behold, the kingdom of God is in your midst." (Luke 17:21b)

Reflect on the past few months for a moment. Have you seen God in your midst? Perhaps He has been guiding you through some difficult circumstances—or maybe you have felt His nearness in a friend's care or a particular Scripture passage. How have you sensed His presence?

______________________________________________

______________________________________________

______________________________________________

______________________________________________

What has He been teaching you?

______________________________________________

______________________________________________

______________________________________________

______________________________________________

If you need a reminder that He is near and is working on your behalf, bask in the light of the following Scriptures. How do they encourage you?

Romans 16:25a ______________________________

______________________________________________

Ephesians 2:14–22 ___________________________

______________________________________________

Philippians 1:6______________________________

______________________________________________

1 Thessalonians 5:23–24 ________________________________

________________________________________________

1 John 3:1–2 ______________________________________

________________________________________________

Jude 24 __________________________________________

________________________________________________

## *Living Insights* STUDY TWO

> "Remember Lot's wife. Whoever seeks to keep his life shall lose it, and whoever loses his life shall preserve it." (Luke 17:32–33)

Have you ever wondered what Lot's wife hoped to see when she looked back at Sodom? Perhaps she was looking for a part of herself in the burning rubble—the part that remained behind because it was still clinging to the comforts and pleasures of this world. That is why God judged her, because she had not surrendered herself completely to Him.

Jesus' theme of clinging to God rather than the world's passing pleasures resonates through Luke's gospel. Block out some time (this may take a little longer than usual) to review what you've learned about this theme so far and to peer ahead in the gospel as well. Note what God may be telling you through Jesus' words.

Luke 6:20–26: What does this passage reveal about priorities?

________________________________________________

________________________________________________

Luke 9:23–25: What does this say about the soul's value?

________________________________________________

________________________________________________

Luke 12:15–21: What meets the soul's needs?

Luke 12:22–34: What attitude is best for the heart?

Luke 14:12–14: What kind of return should we look for in our investments?

Luke 16:9–15, 19–31: What is highly esteemed by the world but detestable to God?

Luke 17:31–33: What does this passage teach about perspective?

Luke 18:18–25: Why do you think Jesus said it is hard for the wealthy to enter the kingdom of God?

Luke 21:34–36: How does this help you understand Jesus' teaching on what to cling to and what to hold loosely?

Chapter 4

# YOU WANT TO BE GODLY? START HERE

*Luke 18:1–17*

Have you ever seen one of those arcade machines that supposedly measures your romantic appeal? Insert a quarter, squeeze the handle, and watch the machine come to life. Lights race and blink like the bulbs on a Hollywood marquee. How far up the scale will you score? *Amorous? Irresistible?* Finally, the indicator comes to rest. *Cold fish*. What? This thing must be broken!

Imagine if God designed a machine that rated us spiritually. What categories would be on His scale?

Certainly, at the bottom would be *hypocrite*. Moving up, we might find *lukewarm*, *little one*, and *overcomer*. What word might denote the highest level of spirituality? *Pious? Saint?* How about this: *godly*.

Every serious Christian longs for the light of godliness to turn on in his or her life. Yet, no matter how hard we try, we never seem to measure up to our image of a godly person. We often have trouble even drawing a clear picture of what godliness looks like.

Is it the gaunt monk in robe and sandals, praying in his room under a halo of moonlight? Or the effervescent preacher, proclaiming the Lord in front of a large congregation? Or the little lady with a warm smile and a worn Bible who sits in the front pew every Sunday? What do you think godliness looks like?

## Random Thoughts and Scriptures on Godliness

Let's set some perimeters around this elusive concept.

### *Some Things It Is . . . and Isn't*

Godliness is *God-likeness*. More specifically, it is *Christ-likeness*. We are "godly" when we allow God to reproduce the character of His Son in us.

The lines of definition blur, however, when we try to trace them in our lives. How consistently must we display Christ's character in order to say, "I'm godly"? Does one slip of the tongue disqualify us? Surely, godly people can't always control what they say or think.

Godliness isn't perfection. Just flip through a few pages in the lives of the saints, and you'll find sinful smudges—some red with innocent blood, as in David's case. He stole a man's wife for a night of pleasure, then had the man killed to cover his sin (2 Sam. 11). Yet, in spite of his moral failure, David was still considered a man after God's heart (Acts 13:22).

What can we conclude? That when godly people make mistakes, they own up to them . . . they don't spend a lifetime hiding them, blaming others, or pretending they never failed (compare 2 Sam. 12:13; Ps. 51). Perfection is Christ's domain; authenticity is ours.

### *What God Says about It . . . and Doesn't Say*

According to Scripture, godliness is achievable. Paul doesn't mock us when he writes, "Be imitators of God" (Eph. 5:1a). While godliness is attainable, though, it isn't automatic. He also writes, "Discipline yourself for the purpose of godliness" (1 Tim. 4:7b).

R. Kent Hughes, in his book *Disciplines of a Godly Man*, explains that Paul's Greek word for *discipline* comes from *gumnos*, from which we derive our English word *gymnasium*. It is

> a word with the smell of the gym in it—the sweat of a good workout. "Gymnasticize (exercise, work out, train) yourself for the purpose of godliness" conveys the feel of what Paul is saying. . . .
>
> In a word, he is calling for some *spiritual sweat!*[1]

Nothing worthwhile comes without effort. That is never more true than in the spiritual realm.

## Jesus Targets Three Specifics

In Luke 18, we can see from Jesus' words three good places to start in any godliness training program. So slip on your gym clothes and lace up your tennis shoes. Let's get at it!

### *Persistence in Prayer*

As the chapter opens, Jesus tells a parable that emphasizes the godly quality of *persistence in prayer*. To develop this, we need to

1. R. Kent Hughes, *Disciplines of a Godly Man* (Wheaton, Ill.: Crossway Books, 1991), p. 16. In 1 Corinthians 9:26–27, Paul describes his spiritual training regimen: "I run in such a way, as not without aim; I box in such a way, as not beating the air; but I buffet my body and make it my slave."

tone up the muscle of *perseverance*. Let's join Jesus now and listen to His story.

> Now He was telling them a parable to show that at all times they ought to pray and not to lose heart, saying, "There was in a certain city a judge who did not fear God, and did not respect man. And there was a widow in that city, and she kept coming to him, saying, 'Give me legal protection from my opponent.'" (vv. 1–3)

This judge's gavel never banged out of respect for God or compassion for the oppressed.[2] Yet the widow never gave up. Every morning, she was first in line at his bench. Every evening, she waited for him at the door, pleading her case. Eventually, the judge said to himself:

> "'Even though I do not fear God nor respect man, yet because this widow bothers me, I will give her legal protection, lest by continually coming she wear me out.'" (vv. 4–5)

The Greek for "wear me out" is literally "give me a black eye." The judge finally granted her request, not out of a sense of fairness or compassion, but for self-preservation.

Jesus brings home His point in the next three verses:

> And the Lord said, "Hear what the unrighteous judge said; now shall not God bring about justice for His elect, who cry to Him day and night, and will He delay long over them? I tell you that He will bring about justice for them speedily.[3] However, when the Son of Man comes, will He find faith on the earth?" (vv. 6–8)

2. "Such judges were notorious," according to William Barclay. "Unless a plaintiff had influence and money to bribe his way to a verdict he had no hope of ever getting his case settled. . . . The widow . . . , without resource of any kind, had no hope of ever extracting justice from such a judge. But she had one weapon—persistence." *The Gospel of Luke*, rev. ed., The Daily Study Bible Series (Philadelphia, Pa.: Westminster Press, 1975), p. 222.

3. According to commentator E. Earle Ellis, the word *speedily* means "suddenly, with the time left indefinite. Although God tarries, when he acts he will act swiftly as he did at the Flood and at Sodom." *The Gospel of Luke*, rev. ed., New Century Bible Commentary Series (1974; reprint, Grand Rapids, Mich.: William B. Eerdmans Publishing Co., 1983), p. 213.

Prayer is not a one-hundred-yard dash—one fast and flashy effort. Rather, Christ shows that it's a marathon of slow and steady petitions. In fact, He invites us to *bother* Him with our requests. To keep asking . . . keep seeking . . . keep knocking (see Matt. 7:7). Or as Paul put it, to "pray without ceasing" (1 Thess. 5:17).

Why does He desire our persistent prayers? Because they demonstrate faith (Luke 18:8b). That's what He's really after. Without faith, prayer is little more than a lucky rabbit's foot that we rub and wonder, "Is it working?" When we pray like that, and an answer finally comes, we're amazed.[4] Godly people, however, pray fervently and believingly—no matter what. They never give up on God. And His answers are merely confirmation of what they've known all along.

### *Acceptance of Others*

A second godly quality is *acceptance of others*, which can be ours as we exercise the spiritual muscle of *humility*. To illustrate this idea, Jesus addresses His next words to

> certain ones who trusted in themselves that they were righteous, and viewed others with contempt. (v. 9)

Sounds like a Pharisee, doesn't it? How fitting, then, that a Pharisee, along with a tax-gatherer, plays a starring role in Jesus' story.

> "Two men went up into the temple to pray, one a Pharisee, and the other a tax-gatherer. The Pharisee stood and was praying thus to himself, 'God, I thank Thee that I am not like other people: swindlers, unjust, adulterers, or even like this tax-gatherer. I fast twice a week; I pay tithes of all that I get.'" (vv. 10–12)

Did you notice whom the Pharisee prayed to? "To himself" (v. 11). This man's heart was bloated with pride. And it naturally follows that the more impressed we are with ourselves, the more judgmental we are of others. The tax-gatherer, however, reveals the opposite attitude.

> "But the tax-gatherer, standing some distance away, was even unwilling to lift up his eyes to heaven, but

4. See the almost comical response of Peter's friends when God answered their prayers in Acts 12:1–17.

> was beating his breast, saying, 'God, be merciful to me, the sinner!' I tell you, this man went down to his house justified rather than the other; for everyone who exalts himself shall be humbled, but he who humbles himself shall be exalted." (vv. 13–14)

The Pharisee was so full of himself that he had no room for God. But the tax-gatherer, a swindler who was ostracized by "decent" people, held out his cup of spiritual poverty and received the riches of God's grace.

Do you want to be godly? Start here, in the training room of the humble, where acknowledging our need of God's mercy and accepting others are the most important parts of the course.

### *Tolerance for Children*

Last, Jesus models a third characteristic of godliness, *tolerance for children*—a quality that exercises our *patience*.

> And they were bringing even their babies to Him so that He might touch them, but when the disciples saw it, they began rebuking them. But Jesus called for them, saying, "Permit the children to come to Me, and do not hinder them, for the kingdom of God belongs to such as these. Truly I say to you, whoever does not receive the kingdom of God like a child shall not enter it at all." (vv. 15–17)

It was customary for mothers to bring their year-old babies to a distinguished rabbi to be blessed.[5] Figuring that Jesus had more pressing matters on His mind, though, the disciples attempted to protect Him from the flow of visitors. But He opened His arms to children of all ages, because they modeled kingdom values—persistence, trust, and honesty.

How often do we brush children aside as interruptions when God has given them to us as lessons about life. Their laughter teaches us about joy. Their eyes guide us into the wonder of God's creation. Their hands reaching for ours show us the kind of faith our Father awaits from us. Only through their kind of faith, openness, and joy, Christ says, will we be able to enter God's eternal kingdom.

5. Barclay, *The Gospel of Luke*, p. 225. The Greek word for "babies" in verse 15 is *brephos*. Jesus used the word *paidion* in verse 16 to include children of all ages.

## Some Practical Ways to Change

This passage teaches us three things to stop doing and three things to start doing if we want to be godly: (1) We must stop bothering others with our complaints and start "bothering" God with our concerns. (2) We must stop impressing others with our piety and start asking God for mercy. (3) We must stop thinking of children as being in the way and start thinking of them as models of the way we should look toward God.

Putting these lessons into practice will take some discipline—some "spiritual sweat." But remember, God isn't expecting perfection. He's just looking for people who are authentic, who admit when they make mistakes, and who are willing to try again.

## *Living Insights* STUDY ONE

What is it that calls a person to roll out of bed before dawn on a Saturday morning, drive miles out of town, and sit for hours in a dinghy on a chilly lake . . . holding a fishing pole . . . watching a bobber twitch . . . eating warm bologna sandwiches?

The same thing that keeps a person casting the same prayer into heaven day after day after day—*perseverance*.

Are you a persevering fisherman when it comes to prayer? Or do you tend to call it a day after a few fruitless casts?

If you feel like giving up, remember the widow pleading with the judge every day. Remember Abraham longing his whole life for his son Isaac to be born. Remember the Hebrew slaves crying out to God those many years in Egypt.

Ever since the beginning, perseverance has been a part of God's godliness training program—it's the only way we can grow in our faith.

What has been your longtime prayer?

____________________________________________________________

____________________________________________________________

In the following space, express to the Lord your commitment to keep casting this request to Him no matter how long it takes to reel in an answer.

____________________________________________________________

________________________________________

________________________________________

________________________________________

## *Living Insights* STUDY TWO

Do you remember the expression, "Cleanliness is next to godliness"? My mother used to say that to get me to wash with soap before supper. I didn't really know what it meant then; and to be honest, I still don't see the connection between clean hands and a godly life. But I have come to realize that, spiritually speaking, cleanliness is a good metaphor for godliness.

When God washes us in His mercy, forgiveness, and grace, we are cleansed from our sins. Guilt and shame stream away; and a fresh, clean conscience is ours.

The tax-gatherer experienced this cleansing when he confessed his sins, depended on God's mercy, and "went down to his house justified" (Luke 18:14). The praying Pharisee, however, mistakenly believed that his righteousness was as good as God's; so he stayed in the filth of his sins.

To be truly godly—truly clean—requires that we humble ourselves before God, strip off all pretenses, stand naked before Him, and let Him scrub away.

Do you, like the tax-gatherer, want God's cleansing? What areas of your life most need His tender mercy?

________________________________________

________________________________________

________________________________________

Are you shivering a little, wondering if God will really do this for you? Let Him reassure you Himself as He speaks to you from His Word.

Hebrews 9:13–14 ________________________________

________________________________________

________________________________________

Hebrews 10:22 ____________________________________________

________________________________________________________

________________________________________________________

1 John 1:7 ______________________________________________

________________________________________________________

________________________________________________________

Revelation 22:14 ________________________________________

________________________________________________________

________________________________________________________

Chapter 5

# Rich Man, Poor Man, Son of Man . . . Me

*Luke 18:18–43*

She was blind, yet she could see a world of beauty that most people miss. She was deaf, yet she could hear the whispered strains of truth in the simplest things. For a long time, she could not speak, yet her life formed words of inspiration that still ring loud and clear.

Her name was Helen Keller.

As a baby, Helen suffered an illness that banished her to a dark and silent dungeon where she could feel but not express, touch but not understand. It was her teacher and lifelong friend, Anne Sullivan, who embraced her with love and rescued her with the lifeline of language.

Her newfound ability to connect with the world made it possible for her to say,

> I can see, and that is why I can be happy, in what you call the dark, but which to me is golden. I can see a God-made world, not a manmade world.[1]

In the last half of Luke 18, Jesus speaks to a rich man, a blind man, and His disciples. Master communicator that He is, He seeks to educate them with the truth and liberate them from their darkness. Whether He succeeds will depend on one thing: their ability to see as Helen Keller saw—through eyes of faith, not eyes of flesh.

## Jesus with a Rich Ruler

The winding path of Jesus' three-and-a-half-year ministry has led Him down this final highway to the Cross. He now approaches Jerusalem through Jericho, a sun-ripened city bursting with the juices of commerce and history. While on His way to Jericho, Jesus meets "a certain ruler" (Luke 18:18a). According to Matthew, he is a "young man," and Mark says that he runs up and kneels before Jesus (Matt. 19:20; Mark 10:17). All three writers agree—this man is rich.

1. Helen Keller, as quoted in *Simpson's Contemporary Quotations*, comp. James B. Simpson (Boston, Mass.: Houghton Mifflin Co., 1988), p. 190.

### *Critical Questions and Answers*

He asks the Lord, "Good Teacher, what shall I do to inherit eternal life?" (Luke 18:18b). Accustomed to formal greetings, the young ruler extends Jesus the title "Good Teacher." But Jesus stops him short and tells him what "good" really means.

> "Why do you call Me good? No one is good except God alone." (v. 19)

Pointing to heaven, Jesus establishes the infinite standard the ruler must achieve. Next, He points to the Law, to illustrate the impossible requirement he must meet.

> "You know the commandments, 'Do not commit adultery, Do not murder, Do not steal, Do not bear false witness, Honor your father and mother.'" (v. 20)

These commands, interestingly, come from the latter half of the Ten Commandments, which deal with our interpersonal relationships. The young man, with the pride that comes from working so hard to be a good person, earnestly proclaims, "All these things I have kept from my youth" (v. 21).

He may have tried with all his might to keep the Law, but being human, he was bound to fail. However, he seems blind to his failures and limited in his grasp of the Law's deep scope. Without arguing the man's claim of goodness, Jesus gives him one more command, one more chance to open his eyes to his own spiritual poverty.

> And when Jesus heard this, He said to him, "One thing you still lack; sell all that you possess, and distribute it to the poor, and you shall have treasure in heaven; and come, follow Me." But when he had heard these things, he became very sad; for he was extremely rich. (vv. 22–23)

Mark says that "at these words his face fell" (Mark 10:22). Jesus has touched the gilded idol of his life: possessions. He has stirred the man out of his dreamy delusion of goodness and awakened him to the glaring reality of his sin.[2]

2. The rich young ruler thought he had kept the Law since his youth, but through his idolatrous materialism, he had broken the first and second commandments: "You shall have no other gods before Me" and "You shall not make for yourself an idol" (Exod. 20:3–4).

### *Confronting Materialism and Greed*

Does the rich man love God as much as he thought? Is he willing to throw his idol of wealth on the fire and follow Jesus? Where will he place his security? In his riches or in Christ? Jesus comments on the struggle within the man's soul:

> "How hard it is for those who are wealthy to enter the kingdom of God! For it is easier for a camel to go through the eye of a needle, than for a rich man to enter the kingdom of God." (Luke 18:24–25)

Can you imagine a camel trying to squeeze through the eye of a needle? First, it crams its slobbery lips through, then its nose, then . . . it's impossible! Just as impossible as one whose heart is set on earthly wealth squeezing himself into the heavenly kingdom.

The disciples are shocked. "Then who can be saved?" they ask (v. 26). Jesus responds with comfort:

> "The things impossible with men are possible with God." (v. 27)

Commentator Leon Morris enriches our understanding of this exchange:

> It was commonly held that riches were a sign of God's blessing, so that the rich man had the best opportunity of the good things of the next world as of this. . . . If the rich with all their advantages can scarcely be saved, what hope is there for others? Jesus makes it clear that there is none. But what man cannot do God can. Salvation, for rich or poor, is always a miracle of divine grace. It is always God's gift.[3]

### *Calming Words of Reassurance*

As Peter watches the rich man denied entrance into the kingdom, he considers his own worthiness. He and the other disciples have trusted Christ. They have left their homes to follow Him (v. 28). Is that enough? Jesus puts an arm of reassurance around them:

3. Leon Morris, *The Gospel according to St. Luke*, The Tyndale New Testament Commentaries Series (Grand Rapids, Mich.: William B. Eerdmans Publishing Co., 1974), p. 268.

> "Truly I say to you, there is no one who has left house or wife or brothers or parents or children, for the sake of the kingdom of God, who shall not receive many times as much at this time and in the age to come, eternal life." (vv. 29–30)

It's amazing how the Lord knows exactly what we need to hear, whether we're the misguided young ruler or the anxious disciples. What can we learn from Jesus' interaction with these people? *When we don't know what we want, but we know something's missing . . . let God educate.* He will make our true need clear to us. Our part, then, is to trust Him and obey.

## Jesus with a Blind Beggar

Let's save for last what Jesus says to His disciples in verses 31–34 and next consider His encounter with a blind beggar on the outskirts of Jericho.

### *A Call for Help*

How different from the rich man is the tattered beggar in this scene. He rules no one. Owns nothing. Bears no mark of goodness. Yet the blind man sees what the rich man could not. He recognizes his need and, with the eyes of faith, looks to the only One who can save him.

> And it came about that as He was approaching Jericho, a certain blind man was sitting by the road, begging. Now hearing a multitude going by, he began to inquire what this might be. And they told him that Jesus of Nazareth was passing by. (vv. 35–37)

As Jesus nears Jericho, a large parade forms—a royal cavalcade. Runners race ahead, heralding the news. A bit of it tumbles into the blind beggar's cup. Someone's coming. Who? Who is it? Jesus of Nazareth!

He has heard about this Jesus—Healer of diseases, Light of the world. He smells the rising cloud of dust. He hears the crescendo of voices. But which voice in this swift current is His? As the crowd washes over him, the man starts to drown in the swirling mass of people. Somewhere in the darkness is his Savior. But *where?*

> And he called out, saying, "Jesus, Son of David,[4] have mercy on me!" And those who led the way were sternly telling him to be quiet; but he kept crying out all the more, "Son of David, have mercy on me!" (vv. 38–39)

At first, he *calls out*, but when they try to hush him, he *cries out*—which is a different word in the Greek. William Barclay describes it as "the instinctive shout of ungovernable emotion, a scream, an almost animal cry."[5] A lifetime of heartache goes into that cry. A lifetime of groping in the darkness and grubbing for food, of being told to shut up and stand aside.

Jesus hears the cry, but more importantly, He hears the pain. He stops the procession and commands those trying to keep him away to lead the blind man to Him (v. 40).

### *A Response to Need*

The turbulent crowd holds its breath as the beggar approaches the King. Jesus speaks first, not as royalty to a subject but as brother to brother. "What do you want Me to do for you?" (v. 41a). Jesus knows the man's need, but He wants *him* to name it.

> And he said, "Lord, I want to regain my sight!" And Jesus said to him, "Receive your sight; your faith has made you well." And immediately he regained his sight, and began following Him, glorifying God; and when all the people saw it, they gave praise to God. (vv. 41b–43)

What the rich man could not do—admit his need and pray for mercy—the blind man did. In response, Jesus went beyond education to liberation. The lesson we learn is this: *When we know what we need but we can't change our situation . . . let God liberate*. Perhaps you've seen someone bound by the chains of addiction or an emotional wound come to Christ and find release. Sometimes it's

4. "Son of David" was a title full of hope for the Messiah's reign (see Isa. 9:6–7; 11:1–12:6; Jer. 23:5–6; 33:14–18; Amos 9:11; Zech. 12:8). William Barclay says that even "the simple people" called Jesus by this name, especially "when they desired the help of [messianic] power for themselves, . . . they were clearly greeting him as the long-expected Messiah." *Jesus as They Saw Him* (1962; reprint, Grand Rapids, Mich.: William B. Eerdmans Publishing Co., 1980), p. 41.

5. William Barclay, *The Gospel of Luke*, rev. ed., The Daily Study Bible Series (Philadelphia, Pa.: Westminster Press, 1975), p. 232.

instantaneous; most often it takes time. But with His help, freedom can be found.

## Jesus with Disillusioned Disciples

Now we come to the middle section of the passage. On one side stands the self-exalted rich man; on the other, the humble beggar. In the center falls the shadow of the Cross.

> And He took the twelve aside and said to them, "Behold, we are going up to Jerusalem, and all things which are written through the prophets about the Son of Man will be accomplished. For He will be delivered to the Gentiles, and will be mocked and mistreated and spit upon, and after they have scourged Him, they will kill Him; and the third day He will rise again." And they understood none of these things, and this saying was hidden from them, and they did not comprehend the things that were said. (vv. 31–34)

This is Jesus' third direct prediction of His passion and resurrection (see 9:21–22, 43b–45), not to mention His many hints about it (see 5:35; 12:50; 13:32–33; 17:25). Why were the disciples so blind? Barclay explains:

> They were obsessed with the idea of a conquering king; they still clung to that hope that he would let loose his power in Jerusalem and blast his enemies off the face of the earth. Here is a great warning to every listener. The human mind has a way of listening only to what it wants to hear. *There are none so blind as those who refuse to see.*[6] (emphasis added)

The lesson we learn is this: *When we can't understand what is happening, but we realize it's out of our control . . . let God be God.*

Let God educate. Let God liberate. Let God be God. To see, we must be willing to open our eyes to all that God might be showing us. His plan is full of the unexpected. It supersedes our own. It may even appear unfair or unwise. But if we can see through the eyes of faith, we can rest in His sovereignty.

6. Barclay, *The Gospel of Luke*, p. 231.

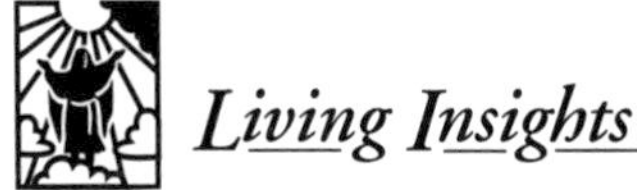

## *Living Insights*

STUDY ONE

The rich ruler made the mistake of coming to Jesus with a clipboard in his hand, seeking a checklist of the things he needed to do to make God happy. What was the reward he sought for a job well done? Eternal life.

Jesus responded with a crash course in how to relate to God. His command that the young man sell his possessions and follow Him was essentially an invitation to a relationship. "Rid yourself of that seductive mistress Money," Jesus was saying, "and love Me with your whole heart."

From time to time, we also need a refresher course in relating to God—especially when life gets hectic and we slip into a maintenance mode with all of our relationships.

Have you simply been "maintaining" God lately? Hoping that worship on Sunday and a few prayers during the week will keep Him satisfied? What has your relationship with Him been like?

_______________________________________________

_______________________________________________

_______________________________________________

_______________________________________________

_______________________________________________

Have any "mistresses" been stealing your love away from Him? If so, what are they?

_______________________________________________

_______________________________________________

_______________________________________________

_______________________________________________

Why don't you take a few minutes to talk to the Lord. Just talk. Don't feel like you need to follow some detailed prayer guideline. Let Him know how much you love Him. Let Him know that He still has your heart.

## *Living Insights*



Think of the ironies in this passage from Luke.

The respected young ruler, who would be ushered to the seat of honor in any synagogue, gets turned away at the gates of heaven.

A blind beggar sees what seminary-trained Pharisees keep missing—Jesus, as the Son of David.

The Jewish Messiah, who is supposed to conquer the Gentiles, is going to be mocked, mistreated, spit upon, scourged, and crucified . . . by the Gentiles.

Ironies.

From beginning to end, Jesus' ministry has brimmed with unexpected turnarounds. The greatest twist of all will be the last, when the sinless One will suffer, and sinners will go free.

Woven into the ironies of the gospel is always that thread of hope—the same hope that inspired Paul to believe the paradox: "When I am weak, then I am strong" (2 Cor. 12:10). The same hope that moved Helen Keller to call her darkness "golden," because it helped her see "a God-made world, not a manmade world."

What is your weakness, your blindness? Could it be that your greatest limitation cradles your greatest strength, because it drives you to depend on the Savior? Could it be that whatever binds you in one respect, liberates you in another?

Jesus specializes in ironies. They lie at the heart of the gospel—a story filled with blind beggars who see.

Chapter 6

# Seeking the Sinner, Saving the Lost

*Luke 19:1–10*

When Steven Spielberg made *Schindler's List*, his penetrating film depicting the horrors of the Holocaust, he wanted us to feel the intensity of the drama as if we were living it. So he determined to use only natural camera angles. No shots from cranes high above the action. No contrived perspectives that detach the viewer from the scene.

In the same way, Luke has "filmed" his gospel from straight-on, eye-level angles. From Jesus' birth in a stable to His death on a cross, Luke gives us a picture of Jesus we can see and touch. What else would we expect from a physician, who has seen and touched the best and worst in the human condition?

Luke's Jesus is a Physician too, forever on call, ready to aid the hurting who cry out to Him from the side of the road. He is the embodiment of divine mercy, reaching out to the outcast, offering hope to the hopeless, seeking and saving the lost.

In our previous lesson, a blind beggar experienced Mercy's touch. In Luke 19, a rich tax collector will be next. The two, though at opposite ends of the social scale, are not as different as we might think. Both are despised, both are lost, and both desperately yearn to be found.

## A True Story of a Sinner's Interest

The procession of people eager to see Jesus had rushed into Jericho like a mighty river, splashing and flowing with energetic praise to God.

### *The Setting*

In his book *Intimate Moments with the Savior,* Ken Gire describes Jericho and its wealth:

> Jericho. Surrounded by palms. Scented with balsam groves. Dates, palm-honey, myrrh, and balsam form a continuous caravan of exports to the East.

> For the Roman government, the city is a lush center of taxation. Plump. Ripe. Fragrant with revenue.
>
> And knee-deep in the harvest are the tax collectors, making sure the proper due is rendered unto Caesar, and in the process, a denarius or two rendered unto themselves.[1]

Tax collectors in Jesus' day were government-sanctioned crooks, thugs in silk suits who arm-twisted merchants into handing over their hard-earned profits. Often, they falsified the tax bills and skimmed off the extra for themselves. One of the heads of the Jericho Mafia was Zaccheus. He was "a chief tax-gatherer," Luke says—and adds the obvious, "he was rich" (Luke 19:2).

The finest clothes lined his closets. He wore ruby and emerald rings on his fingers like golden bands on fat cigars, and he liked to wave them under people's noses when he talked. He was a prosperous businessman. He could buy anything his heart desired—anything, that is, but self-respect and the friendship of others.

The same road that had led him to the pinnacle of success had dead-ended him in the back alley of loneliness and isolation. People despised tax collectors, and they despised him. He had everything, yet his heart was as empty as a widow's cupboard.

Perhaps that realization is what drew him to Jesus. Here was a man who owned nothing of this world, yet possessed the love and admiration of thousands. And Zaccheus had even heard that He was a friend of tax-gatherers! If he could just get one glimpse of this man, maybe he could see in Him what he lacked.

As the procession passed by, Zaccheus "was trying to see who Jesus was, and he was unable because of the crowd, for he was small in stature" (v. 3). Did we mention that Zaccheus was short? This limitation had never stopped him from getting what he wanted before, and now he yearned to see Jesus more than anything. Determined,

> he ran on ahead and climbed up into a sycamore tree in order to see Him, for He was about to pass through that way. (v. 4)

### *The Seeking*

We may marvel at this little rich man in his fine robes shinnying

1. Ken Gire, *Intimate Moments with the Savior* (Grand Rapids, Mich.: Zondervan Publishing House, 1989), p. 73.

up a sycamore tree to see Jesus. More remarkable than that, though, was what Jesus did. In the moment it took Him to catch sight of Zaccheus among the branches, He read the secret lines of heartache etched in his soul. Once again, Jesus stopped the procession to seek the lost sinner.

> And when Jesus came to the place, He looked up and said to him, "Zaccheus, hurry and come down, for today I must stay at your house." And he hurried and came down, and received Him gladly. (vv. 5–6)

In the same way that Jesus gave sight to a blind beggar, He gave dignity and friendship to a despised tax collector. First, He called Zaccheus by name. Then He bestowed on him the highest of honors—He expressed a desire to stay at his house. He wanted to get to know Zaccheus on his turf. He wanted to talk to him in the privacy of his home, away from the eavesdropping crowd.

Zaccheus must have felt ten feet tall as Jesus walked with him past the Pharisees to his home. Jesus' critics, though, stood at a distance with their arms folded.

> And when they saw it, they all began to grumble, saying, "He has gone to be the guest of a man who is a sinner." (v. 7)

Most likely, the next verse describes what happened after dinner. Zaccheus "stopped," or more accurately, "stood," and announced to the Lord,

> "Behold, Lord, half of my possessions I will give to the poor, and if I have defrauded anyone of anything, I will give back four times as much." (v. 8)

Ken Gire describes the amazing transformation of this man whose life was once stunted by greed but now flows with generosity.

> From behind the barriers he has erected around his heart, a flood of repentant feelings bursts forth. Feelings that had been dammed up for years. Zacchaeus goes out on still another limb. What took a lifetime to accumulate, one sentence of devotion liquidates. And not by a token ten percent. Half to the poor. Fourfold to the defrauded.
>
> Look closely. Witness the miracle—a camel

> passing through the eye of a needle.[2]

*The Saving*

Seeing the evidence of his faith, Jesus assured Zaccheus: "Today salvation has come to this house, because he, too, is a son of Abraham" (v. 9).

Jesus' promise must have lifted Zaccheus like wind under eagles' wings, sending his self-respect soaring.

What can we learn from Jesus' words to this repentant sinner? First, any person who has been saved can be assured of that salvation immediately. And once a person is saved, the evidence will be a changed life, as with Zaccheus making amends for his cheating. Also, the first ones to notice those changes will often be a person's family—"salvation has come to *this house*."

Closing the scene, Christ utters the words we've identified as the theme of Luke's gospel. It's fitting that it should appear here in the book, right after Jesus has saved the poor beggar and the rich tax-collector, and right before His final approach to Jerusalem and the Cross:

> "For the Son of Man has come to seek and to save that which was lost." (v. 10)

## A Personal Response to the Savior's Mission

Whenever you feel lost, remember the verse above. And remember the following two principles.

*The Lord seeks us far more intensely than we seek Him.* In John's gospel, Jesus reminds His disciples, "You did not choose Me, but I chose you" (John 15:16; see also Rom. 5:6–8). We respond by saying yes to Him, but He is the initiator. He calls our name, like He called Zaccheus; He offers the invitation. Our part is to welcome and receive.

*The Lord saves those who acknowledge they're sinners, not those who think they're saints.* We can pretend we're found. We can play the part of a saint and convince even ourselves. But Christ isn't looking for nice, wholesome people who don't think they need Him. Earlier in His ministry, He said, "I have not come to call the righteous but sinners to repentance" (Luke 5:32). He's searching for the "chief" sinners, those who know their lives are empty without Him.

2. Gire, *Intimate Moments with the Savior,* p. 76.

## *Living Insights* STUDY ONE

Lost in the woods, Hansel and Gretel trudge for hours, hoping to find their way home. By nightfall, though, they are only farther into the forest. With nothing to eat, they huddle together, shivering through the dark and frightful night. The next morning, hunger gnawing their stomachs, they set out again. On the verge of despair, they spy a little bird that leads them to a clearing in the forest. Rubbing their eyes, they gaze upon the most wonderful house they have ever seen. Instead of wood, it is made of bread, with scrumptious cakes for a roof and transparent sugar for windows.

Coming near, Hansel breaks off a piece of the roof and tastes it. Gretel tries a bit of the window. Delicious! Just then, they hear a thin voice from inside,

> Nibble, nibble, like a mouse,
> Who is nibbling at my house?

We all know whose voice it is, don't we? Hansel and Gretel think they're saved, but really they have stumbled upon a witch's house and are in more danger than before.

In many ways, Satan is like that witch, and the world with its perks and pleasures is like the house of bread. As long as he can keep us nibbling on sweets, we forget we're lost. For a while, we lose sight of home and our heavenly Father. We don't realize that Satan is merely fattening us up for the kill.

Hansel and Gretel weren't the only ones to discover the witch's house. Wealthy Zaccheus resided there for awhile, feeding on the world's delights, smacking his lips and licking the sugar off his fingers.

Perhaps the witch's luscious house has lured you as well. Attempting to dull the ache of being lost, you've stuffed yourself with the things money can buy. Your life is plush and fat . . . yet, for all the feasting, there's still an emptiness inside. A longing for home.

Jesus seeks and saves those who are *lost*—those who realize Satan's house is not their home. Those like Zaccheus, who sense their need and are willing to go out on a limb to see Him.

Instead of reaching for another piece of worldly cake, reach out to Jesus. Use the following space to reflect on your inner longings and where you've been going to satisfy them. Express to the Lord your feelings of lostness and your deep desire to be found by Him.

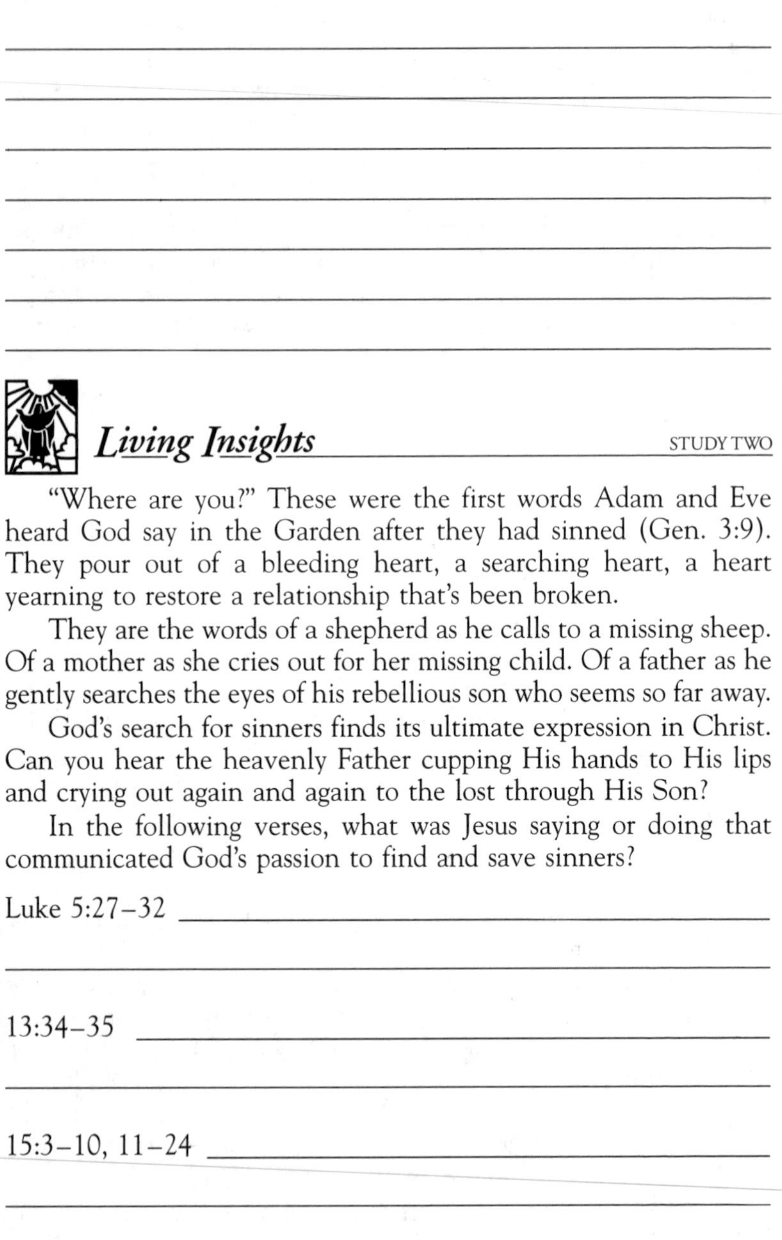

## *Living Insights* STUDY TWO

"Where are you?" These were the first words Adam and Eve heard God say in the Garden after they had sinned (Gen. 3:9). They pour out of a bleeding heart, a searching heart, a heart yearning to restore a relationship that's been broken.

They are the words of a shepherd as he calls to a missing sheep. Of a mother as she cries out for her missing child. Of a father as he gently searches the eyes of his rebellious son who seems so far away.

God's search for sinners finds its ultimate expression in Christ. Can you hear the heavenly Father cupping His hands to His lips and crying out again and again to the lost through His Son?

In the following verses, what was Jesus saying or doing that communicated God's passion to find and save sinners?

Luke 5:27–32 ________________________________

13:34–35 ________________________________

15:3–10, 11–24 ________________________________

18:31–34 ________________________________

If this study in Luke leaves you with only one thought about Christ, this is it: "The Son of Man has come to seek and to save that which was lost" (19:10). Let that verse sink past your mind into the soft folds of your heart.

*The God of creation has come to seek and save me. Through the forest of my sin, into the canyons and across the great deserts, He searches for me. "Where are you?" He cries. Finally, He looks up. And there I am, hiding in the branches of guilt and fear. He calls my name. He invites me to come down. "I must stay with you forever," He says.*

Such great love. Zaccheus couldn't resist it. He welcomed Christ with open arms. Will you?

Chapter 7

# MAKING SENSE WITH YOUR DOLLARS

*Luke 19:11–27*

Predawn, January 17, 1994. Los Angeles is jolted awake by a giant of an earthquake. For forty-five seconds, the titan pounds its fists and stomps its feet in a furious rampage through the city. As the ground trembles, structures jerk up and down and shake apart.

Inside darkened homes, people are thrown out of their beds. Chandeliers dance to an eerie rhythm. Refrigerators lurch across the linoleum. Drawers and cabinet doors fling open, tossing their contents onto the floor in a spray of broken glass. Blinds chatter. Walls split. Foundations crack.

In the aftermath, dazed residents stumble through the blackness, flipping light switches that don't work, testing phones that are dead. They wander outside and wait for the rising sun to reveal the wreckage.

As the earthquake tested the strength of their houses, so the ruins will test the depth of their character. If they have invested their hopes and security in earthly treasures, their lives will lie in shambles among the shards of glass. If they have invested in eternal treasures, they will be shaken but not destroyed. They will be able to say with a fellow earthquake victim, as he put his arm around his wife: "We have lost everything, and yet we really have lost nothing of highest value."

Do you have the kind of perspective on material possessions that will allow you to withstand life's earthquakes, big or small? To develop that perspective, we must begin with a biblical understanding of money.

## When It Comes to Money, Always Remember Three Things . . .

Three foundational principles can reinforce a resilient attitude toward money, especially during shaky times.

### *What You Need Most Cannot Be Purchased with Money*

Consider what money can and cannot buy. Money can buy a bed but not sleep. It can buy pleasure but not peace. Medicine but not health. Companionship but not friendship. A crucifix but not a Savior.[1]

By focusing on money and things, we lose sight of what's most important (see Luke 12:20–21). Topping the list is our salvation, which Peter says was bought not with money but with the precious blood of Christ (1 Pet. 1:18–19).

### *What You Have Has Been Provided by God*

By His grace, God provides us minds to think and backs to work—our very ability to earn a paycheck. Without Him, we'd have nothing. Our houses, our stereos, our cars, even our lives are His property, all on loan to us from His heavenly warehouse (see Luke 12:27–32).

### *What You Spend Is an Expression of Your Priorities*

We spend money on what we consider important. Food and clothing and shelter, as well as schooling and medical care and giving, are all priorities. And all are OK—as long as our hearts are in the right place (see v. 34).

## When Jesus Talked about Money, He Used This Approach . . .

Zaccheus' heart was set right after one meeting with Jesus. Immediately he sold his stock in greed and invested heavily in generosity, his checkbook ledger quickly reflecting his new set of priorities. While the crowd was still grappling with this stunning change, Jesus took the occasion to tell them a parable about money (19:11a).

### *He Had a Reason*

This subject was important to Christ because "He was near Jerusalem," and everyone "supposed that the kingdom of God was going to appear immediately" (v. 11b).

Having caught the kingdom fever that was epidemic in Palestine, the disciples expected Christ to enter Jerusalem as a conquering hero, to vanquish Rome, and to immediately set up God's rule on earth. Even after His resurrection, they were asking Him if now was the time for "restoring the kingdom to Israel" (Acts 1:6). They

1. Adapted from "What Money Can Buy" in *Encyclopedia of 7,7000 Illustrations*, ed. Paul Lee Tan (Chicago, Ill.: Assurance Publishers, 1979), p. 832.

never imagined that Jesus would delay His reigning on earth.

So Jesus tells them this parable about the future and the importance of using their money and resources wisely while they wait for His kingdom.

### *He Told a Story*

The story includes five key elements. The first element is the nobleman, who goes away

> "to a distant country to receive a kingdom for himself, and then return." (Luke 19:12)

The nobleman represents Jesus, who will soon leave for the distant country of heaven. There He will receive His kingdom and eventually return to establish His authority on earth.

Second, there are two groups of people: ten of the nobleman's slaves (v. 13), who represent Christ's followers awaiting His appearing; and the citizens of the country he leaves behind—unbelievers who resist Jesus' rule over their lives (v. 14).

The third element is the money the nobleman leaves with his slaves. He gives each slave one "mina," which equals about one-third of an average worker's yearly salary. The mina represents not only money but also the resources or talents God places in our hands. We all have a calling or a skill and the same twenty-four hours a day to do something with it.

The fourth element is the nobleman's command: "Do business with this until I come back" (v. 13). The slaves have complete freedom to invest his money any way they wish, as long as they make a gain for their master.

The fifth element is ultimate accountability. The nobleman returns as a king and orders

> "that these slaves, to whom he had given the money, be called to him in order that he might know what business they had done." (v. 15)

Jesus doesn't say how long the nobleman was gone, perhaps years. But when he returns, business is on his mind, and he's in charge. He doesn't ask—he orders them forward to give an account of their investments.

How well do the slaves fare?

> "And the first appeared, saying, 'Master, your mina

> has made ten minas more.' And he said to him, 'Well done, good slave, because you have been faithful in a very little thing, be in authority over ten cities.' And the second came, saying, 'Your mina, master, has made five minas.' And he said to him also, 'And you are to be over five cities.'" (vv. 16–19)

Notice, the two slaves refer to the money as "*your* mina." They rightly recognize that the money and profits were his, not theirs. Notice also that the rewards correspond to the returns (vv. 17, 19). No longer slaves, they became rulers of cities.

Then a third slave steps forward to give his report. His reward matches his return too. *Nothing.*

> "And another came, saying, 'Master, behold your mina, which I kept put away in a handkerchief; for I was afraid of you, because you are an exacting man; you take up what you did not lay down, and reap what you did not sow.' He said to him, 'By your own words I will judge you, you worthless slave. Did you know that I am an exacting man, taking up what I did not lay down, and reaping what I did not sow? Then why did you not put the money in the bank, and having come, I would have collected it with interest?'" (vv. 20–23)

Folding the mina in a handkerchief was not the master's idea of doing business. The slave claimed he hid it because he was afraid, but if he really feared the master, he would have obeyed him. Even a safe, low-interest savings account would have been better than nothing.

Displeased with the slave, the master tells those standing near, "Take the mina away from him, and give it to the one who has the ten minas" (v. 24). But they object, "Master, he has ten minas already" (v. 25). The king answers them with a principle and a prediction that points to the heart of Jesus' message.

### *He Included a Principle and a Prediction*

The *principle* is this: You cannot stand still and continue to grow. Jesus says,

> "I tell you, that to everyone who has shall more be given, but from the one who does not have, even what he does have shall be taken away." (v. 26)

We've all heard the phrase, "Use it or lose it." And it's true. An athlete's muscles and skills will atrophy without training; an artist's creativity will shrivel if the imagination isn't stretched. When we go through one door of learning and growth, we're led to more doors and even greater opportunities for growth.

So whatever resources, talents, or interests God has given you, remember—*don't sit on your mina.* And don't worry about how many minas you have, either. The Master is more pleased with less talented believers who use what they have than highly talented believers who do nothing.

The *prediction* concerns the citizens who resisted the nobleman's claim to power (see v. 14). When he returns as king, they will receive judgment that is both swift and grim.

> "But these enemies of mine, who did not want me to reign over them, bring them here and slay them in my presence." (v. 27)

Although they had had no minas to invest, they had possessed the greatest gift any person could have—time. The master had given them plenty of time to submit to his rule while he was gone, but they blew their opportunity. Now it was too late—just as it will be for unbelievers when Christ comes again as King of Kings.

## When We Use the Money God Provides, Never Forget . . .

Any earthquake will look child-size compared to the king-size temblor that will rumble through people's lives when Jesus returns. Let's put in place three principles from the passage that will help us build a firm, quake-proof foundation.

First, *when we use money, it is an investment of God's resources, not ours.* The Lord cares about how we're using His property. He's loaned it to us to earn dividends for His kingdom—to show love, to give encouragement, to transform lives. Be wise in how you handle His gift.

Second, *the Lord will reward broad vision, not fearful restraint.* Fear of failure, criticism, or burnout has caused many of us to sit with our minas neatly folded in napkins, patiently waiting for Christ's return. Jesus, however, commands us to *do business.* So think big. Be generous. And remember, He smiled on the ones who risked.

Third, *we will ultimately give account to the Lord, not others.* All believers will one day stand before Christ's judgment seat—not the judgment seat of our parents, brothers, sisters, bosses, or friends (see 2 Cor. 5:10). People often measure us by standards we can never achieve. But Jesus measures us according to the potential with which He created us.

There's freedom in that thought, isn't there? Freedom to take a chance. Freedom to try. Freedom to invest our lives in things that last.

## *Living Insights* STUDY ONE

"You just used the C-word," said the gymnastics teacher to my preschool son. "That means I'm going to have to tickle you!" My son grinned and covered his tummy as she squeezed a giggle out of him. "Now, what's the *T*-word?"

She had asked him to attempt a maneuver called "skin the cat," which involves hanging from a bar and doing a sort of backward somersault, then reversing the process. He'd considered the plan, then shaken his head. "I *can't*." That was the C-word.

"Now, what's the *T*-word?"

My son hesitated for a moment. "I'll *try*," he said and stepped up to the bar.

Have you been saying the C-word a lot lately? "Lord, I can't use my talent for your glory. I might fall. People might criticize me. I can't perform nearly as well as this other person. I wish I could . . . but I can't."

Hmmm. You may need a good tickling. Better yet, write down the talent you think God wants you to use for His kingdom. Then, if you've been holding on to your "mina," explain to Him what is keeping you from doing business with it.

________________________________________

________________________________________

________________________________________

________________________________________

He understands your fears. But He still wants you to try. What confidence does He give you in 2 Corinthians 12:9–10, Philippians 4:13, and 2 Timothy 1:6–9?

________________________________________

If you decided to use the *T*-word right now, what would be your first step? Your next step? And the step after that?

Are you starting to build some courage? You have a plan. It's time to step up to the bar and give it a try.

## *Living Insights* STUDY TWO

When we borrow a tool or a book from someone most of us take great care to return it promptly and in the same condition—or better. We respect others' property and feel responsible for it.

When it comes to God's property, however, and especially the money He has given us, are we as careful? Are we governed by the same sense of responsible stewardship? To find out, let's evaluate ourselves in light of the following perspectives of God's ownership of everything.

> God has the right to whatever He wants whenever He wants it. It is all His, because an owner has *rights*, and I, as a steward, have only *responsibilities*. . . . I literally possess much but own nothing.[2]

Compare this with the rich young ruler's attitude in Luke 18:18–23. Then ask yourself, Which attitude resembles my own?

2. Ron Blue, *Master Your Money* (Nashville, Tenn.: Thomas Nelson Publishers, 1986), pp. 19–20.

> Not only is my giving decision a spiritual decision, but *every* spending decision is a spiritual decision. There is nothing more spiritual about giving than buying a car, taking a vacation, buying food, paying off debt, paying taxes, and so on. These are all uses of His resources.[3]

Do you *spend* money with the same sense of responsibility toward God that you have when you *give* money? Or does your sense of stewardship extend only as far as tithing?

> You can't fake stewardship. Your checkbook reveals all that you really believe about stewardship. . . . It reflects your goals, priorities, convictions, relationships, and even the use of your time.[4]

Take a look at last month's bank statement. What does it reveal about your attitude toward money? Does it reflect the goals, priorities, and convictions of someone who's a steward? Or an owner?[5]

3. Blue, *Master Your Money*, p. 20.

4. Blue, *Master Your Money*, p. 20.

5. This Living Insight is adapted from the Bible study guide *Strike the Original Match*, coauthored by Lee Hough, from the Bible-teaching ministry of Charles R. Swindoll (Anaheim, Calif.: Insight for Living, 1992), pp. 85–86.

Chapter 8

# UNFORGETTABLE SCENES OF THE SAVIOR

*Luke 19:28–48*

"We are going up to Jerusalem" (Luke 18:31).

Determination resonates in Jesus' voice as He strides forward on the last leg of His life's journey. To mark Jesus' final trip, Luke signposts the craggy seventeen-mile climb from Jericho to Jerusalem with several phrases that build the drama of His approach to the Holy City.

- "As He was approaching Jericho" (18:35)
- "He entered and was passing through Jericho" (19:1)
- "He was going on ahead, ascending to Jerusalem" (v. 28)
- "He approached Bethphage and Bethany, near the mount that is called Olivet"[1] (v. 29)
- "As He was now approaching, near the descent of the Mount of Olives" (v. 37)
- "When He approached, He saw the city" (v. 41)
- "He entered the temple" (v. 45)

Journey's end. The blood of a million sacrifices has called Jesus to this city, this temple, this altar. Here, in just a few days, on the Passover, He will offer Himself as the precious Lamb of God, the supreme sacrifice for our sins.

## Three Significant Events En Route

Three unforgettable scenes chronicle Jesus' arrival in Jerusalem. The emotion of three years of ministry bursts forth in a climactic

1. Bethphage and Bethany are two villages along the Jericho road, located about two miles from Jerusalem. The mount called "Olivet," more often called the Mount of Olives, is a mile-long ridge that overlooks the city from the east.

celebration of joy, a display of heart-wrenching sorrow, and an act of righteous anger.

### *Jesus' Triumphal Entry*

Jesus has entered Jerusalem before—as a boy, as a worshiper, and as a teacher. But never as a king . . . until now.

As He approaches Bethphage and Bethany, He sends two disciples into one of these villages just outside Jerusalem with these instructions:

> "Go into the village opposite you, in which as you enter you will find a colt tied, on which no one yet has ever sat; untie it, and bring it here. And if anyone asks you, 'Why are you untying it?' thus shall you speak, 'The Lord has need of it.'" (vv. 30–31)

The disciples find the colt just as Jesus said they would—right down to the words He gave them. And its owners hand it over to them without a stutter of complaint (vv. 32–35a).

Leading the colt to Jesus, the disciples saddle the animal with their cloaks and set their Master on it (v. 35). It is a sacred task for this small donkey to bear the King of Kings. In war, kings would ride horses, but in peace, they entered the city riding donkeys.[2] This is how Jesus presents Himself to the world—the Messiah of peace. And the crowds join in the triumphant celebration.

> As He was going, they were spreading their garments in the road. And as He was now approaching, near the descent of the Mount of Olives, the whole multitude of the disciples began to praise God joyfully with a loud voice for all the miracles which they had seen, saying,
>
> "Blessed is the King who comes in the name of
> the Lord;
> Peace in heaven and glory in the highest!"
>
> (vv. 36–38)

Throughout Jesus' ministry, He has resisted the king's mantle His followers have been trying to throw around His shoulders (see John 6:15). Why is this Passover different?

2. William Barclay, *The Gospel of Luke*, rev. ed., The Daily Study Bible Series (Philadelphia, Pa.: Westminster Press, 1975), p. 240.

First, Jesus is fulfilling prophecy. Zechariah foretold this moment almost five hundred years earlier:

> Rejoice greatly, O daughter of Zion!
> Shout in triumph, O daughter of Jerusalem!
> Behold, your king is coming to you;
> He is just and endowed with salvation,
> Humble, and mounted on a donkey,
> Even on a colt, the foal of a donkey. (Zech. 9:9)

In his book *Intense Moments with the Savior,* Ken Gire explains a second reason for Jesus' triumphant entry.

> In so coming Jesus forces the hand of the religious aristocracy. After this public act, they would have to cast a public vote. No more meetings behind closed doors. No more plotting in private. They would have to come out in the open. They would have to confess him or curse him. Crown him or kill him.[3]

Jesus is removing all doubt from the religious leaders' minds as to His claims. The multitudes shower Him with praise from the messianic Psalm 118, "Blessed is the one who comes in the name of the Lord" (v. 26)—and He receives it. The sour-faced Pharisees in the crowd are appalled by what they consider blasphemy: "Teacher, rebuke Your disciples"[4] (Luke 19:39). To them, He is a teacher. Nothing more.

Jesus confronts them: "I tell you, if these become silent, the stones will cry out!" (v. 40). Even the rocks along the road recognize Him as the Son of God. Are the Pharisees so stubborn that they can't see the truth and lift their voices too? Are their hearts harder than stone?

### *Weeping over the City*

As Jesus crests the Mount of Olives, the golden city rises before Him. Jerusalem. The name means "city of peace," yet how little peace these walls have witnessed. Over the centuries, God sent His

3. Ken Gire, *Intense Moments with the Savior* (Grand Rapids, Mich.: Zondervan Publishing House, 1994), p. 72.

4. The Pharisees dare not attempt to silence the crowd themselves—Jesus' popularity is too great. They must wait for their lies and false accusations to sow seeds of doubt in the people's hearts.

prophets to guide the people to the light, but they returned bloodied and naked, if they returned at all. Now He is offering them their final hope for peace, His only Son.

Looking across the Kidron Valley, Jesus sees the great stone walls of the city, the impregnable towers, and the sheer marble sides of the temple rising like white cliffs from Mount Zion. This is what the people have become toward God—a walled-off fortress. They are the citizens in Jesus' parable of the ten minas, who shake their fists at the king and shout, "We do not want this man to reign over us" (v. 14).

The songs of praise in His ears only heighten His feelings of heartache, for He knows they will soon turn to shouts of rage—"Crucify Him!"—then screams of terror when the Romans ravage the city in A.D. 70. So Luke takes the time to record Jesus' feelings:

> And when He approached, He saw the city and wept over it. (v. 41)

These are not the quiet tears of a disappointed dream but the chest-heaving sobs of a parent over a destructively rebellious child (compare 2 Sam. 18:33). They are the tears of a prophet whose heedless people have broken his heart (compare Jer. 9:1). And they are tears of regret—regret for what might have been if only Jerusalem had opened her arms to her Messiah.

> "If you had known in this day, even you, the things which make for peace! But now they have been hidden from your eyes. For the days shall come upon you when your enemies will throw up a bank before you, and surround you, and hem you in on every side, and will level you to the ground and your children within you, and they will not leave in you one stone upon another, because you did not recognize the time of your visitation." (Luke 19:42–44; see also Matt. 23:37–39)

### *Activities in the Temple*

With His heart still raw with grief, Jesus at last enters Jerusalem and heads for the temple. He doesn't stir the crowd with a well-rehearsed speech. Instead, according to Mark's account, He looks around in silence (Mark 11:11a). What does He find at His Father's house of worship? A flea market!

Merchants hawk priest-certified animals for Passover sacrifice. "Make amends for your sins," barks one gravel-voiced trader, "Get your spotless lamb here, tagged and ready for the altar." Money-changers sit behind tables, milking foreign visitors with their exorbitant exchange rates.

Instead of whispered prayers, Jesus hears clinking coins. Instead of incense, He smells the dung of sheep and cattle. Who is behind this exploitative monopoly?

William Barclay says that "these Temple shops were known as the Booths of Annas and were the property of the family of the High Priest."[5] Rather than praying for the people, these hypocritical priests were preying on the people.

Jesus has seen enough. He leaves the city and spends the night in Bethany (Mark 11:11b). The next morning, on Monday, He returns.

> And He entered the temple and began to cast out those who were selling, saying to them, "It is written, 'And My house shall be a house of prayer,' but you have made it a robbers' den." (Luke 19:45–46)

As Jesus' storm strikes, tables crash. Coins skitter across the stone floor. Doves flap in their cages. Bleating sheep bolt for shelter. Merchants scoop up their goods and beat a path to the exit.

This is not the hot-poker rage of an impatient man (compare Eph. 4:26). It is righteous indignation—lightning flashes of God's holiness that burn holes in our filthy garments of sin and cleanse our hearts.

The proud religious leaders, however, are more concerned about maintaining their power and their pocketbooks than examining their hearts. Smoldering with embarrassment at their exposed greed, they plot a way to reduce Jesus to ashes.

> And He was teaching daily in the temple; but the chief priests and the scribes and the leading men among the people were trying to destroy Him, and they could not find anything that they might do, for all the people were hanging upon His words. (Luke 19:47–48)

5. Barclay, *The Gospel of Luke*, p. 242.

## Jesus, Jerusalem, and Us Today

Three scenes. Each captures Jesus in a different light—as a humble king, receiving the praise of His subjects; as a compassionate parent, weeping over His lost children; as an angry judge, fighting for what's right. What can we learn from Jesus' example in these scenes?

First, *courage can be demonstrated as much in our anger as in our compassion*. Sometimes sitting idly and shrugging off the wrongs in this world is the most cowardly thing we can do. As Robert Louis Stevenson once wrote, "the cruelest lies are often told in silence."[6] Getting angry at sin and standing up for the truth can be the most spiritual and courageous thing we do.

Second, *faithfulness is revealed as much in ending well as in continuing strong*. To the very end, Jesus kept on teaching, showing compassion, and confronting sin. He's a model of perseverance.

May the Lord give us the same courage and faithfulness to follow Him no matter what the cost.

## *Living Insights*

STUDY ONE

Jesus doesn't exactly fit the Rambo image of courage as He quietly rides into town on a little donkey. Yet, according to William Barclay, Jesus defined the word *courage* when He entered Jerusalem.

> By this time there was a price on Jesus' head. (John 11:57.) It would have been natural that, if he must go into Jerusalem at all, he should have slipped in unseen and hidden away in some secret place in the back streets. But he entered in such a way as to focus the whole lime-light upon himself and to occupy the centre of the stage. It is a breath-taking thing to think of a man with a price upon his head, an outlaw, deliberately riding into a city in such a way that every eye was fixed upon him. It is impossible to exaggerate the sheer courage of Jesus.[7]

What was one of the first things He did in Jerusalem? Defy and

6. As quoted in *Bartlett's Familiar Quotations*, 15th ed., rev. and enl., ed. Emily Morison Beck (Boston, Mass.: Little, Brown and Co., 1980), p. 667.

7. Barclay, *The Gospel of Luke*, pp. 239–40.

embarrass the most powerful political and religious family, the family of the High Priest, by casting out the sellers in the temple. Then He taught there every day, leading the people away from their false shepherds.

That kind of courage doesn't come naturally. In Ephesians 6:19–20 and Philippians 1:19–20, what did Paul rely on to give him boldness?

_______________________________________________

_______________________________________________

According to 2 Corinthians 5:4–8, what perspective can help remove your fears?

_______________________________________________

_______________________________________________

_______________________________________________

In what areas do you need to follow Christ's example of courage?

_______________________________________________

_______________________________________________

_______________________________________________

_______________________________________________

Courage doesn't mean not feeling any fear; it means going on in spite of it. So stand up for Christ's cause, even if your knees knock. Jesus is right there to steady you.

## *Living Insights* STUDY TWO

Do you wonder whether Jesus felt a crush of rejection when He came home to the temple? This was His Father's house, His family's home. The priests were supposed to remain faithful, yet they had left their God and married the gods of money, power, and prestige. And they had taken His children with them.

Where had the priesthood gone wrong? When did its devotion grow stale? Perhaps during the years of routine religious activity.

Perhaps during some of the elite social functions and sumptuous banquets that their position afforded them.

It happened to the priests in the temple, and it can happen to Christians as well. Take a moment to read Christ's letter to the church at Ephesus in Revelation 2:1–4.

Is there anything you need to talk to God about, in light of this passage? Feel free to use the following space to reestablish your relationship with or express your faithfulness to your First Love. He waits to gather you in His arms (Matt. 23:37).

Chapter 9

# FIGHTING FIRE WITH FIRE

*Luke 20:1–26*

*Scene: Western saloon, dimly lit. Long wooden bar. Wide-angle shot reveals* MARSHAL DILLON *seated on a stool, hunched over a glass. Enter* FESTUS *through swinging doors.*

FESTUS: Matthew? I been lookin' everywhere for you. The James twins have jus' about done tore up this town.

DILLON *gulps down drink. Recoils.*

FESTUS: Well, dadburnit. *(agitated)* Ain't you gonna do anything?

*Enter* DOC.

DOC: Matt, it's looking bad out there. Schoolhouse is on fire. Church is all shot up. And Matt . . . they got Miss Kitty.

DILLON *jumps up, then sits back down.*

DILLON: No. *(determined)* No! This time, I'm not going to fight. I've decided . . . to turn the other cheek.

## The Flip Side of "Turning the Other Cheek"

That's a scene you'd never see on the old *Gunsmoke* television series. But what, then, did Jesus mean when He said, "Whoever hits you on the cheek, offer him the other also" (Luke 6:29a)? As Christians, aren't we supposed to let bullies push us around and never show any backbone?

"That would be ridiculous," writes the sixteenth-century reformer Martin Luther,

> like the case of the crazy saint who let the lice nibble at him and refused to kill any of them on account of this text, maintaining that he had to suffer and could not resist evil.[1]

Turning the other cheek doesn't mean we can't protect ourselves or defend what's right.

1. Martin Luther, *The Sermon on the Mount and the Magnificat*, ed. Jaroslav Pelikan, vol. 21 of Luther's Works (St. Louis, Mo.: Concordia Publishing House, 1956), p. 110.

People often paint Jesus as the paragon of passivity—they can't imagine Him resisting lice either. But that's not the Jesus of the gospels.

In Matthew 15:1–9, Jesus faced down the self-righteous Pharisees. His example teaches us that *there are times when it is necessary to expose the enemy.*

In the next chapter, Jesus stood toe-to-toe with Peter, who had wrongly rebuked Him: "Get behind Me, Satan! You are a stumbling block to Me; for you are not setting your mind on God's interests, but man's" (v. 23). As Jesus shows, *there are times when we need to confront a friend.*

Finally, as we saw in Luke 19:45–46, Jesus threw the money-changers out of the temple with His strong carpenter's hands. He didn't make it a practice to use force, but in this case, the purity of worship was at stake—a principle He was passionate about. Clearly, then, *there are times when it is essential to stand on a principle.*

## The Day Jesus Took His Own Defense

Jesus' cleansing of the temple sets the stage for the final show-down in Jerusalem. The religious leaders have refused to admit their hypocrisy and release their iron grip on the people. So it has come down to either them or Jesus. In Luke 20, they call Him out to fight.

### *Identifying the Resistance*

> And it came about on one of the days while He was teaching the people in the temple and preaching the gospel, that the chief priests and the scribes with the elders confronted Him. (v. 1)

According to William Barclay, the three groups represented here are "the component parts of the Sanhedrin, the supreme council and governing body of the Jews."[2] Earlier, in Luke 9:22, Jesus predicted that these groups would reject Him. Interestingly, the word He used for *reject* means "reject after investigation."[3] Like reporters trailing a controversial politician, they have been watching Him with suspicious eyes, scribbling down His every word to distort and use against Him.

2. William Barclay, *The Gospel of Luke*, rev. ed., The Daily Study Bible Series (Philadelphia, Pa.: Westminster Press, 1975), p. 243.

3. Fritz Rienecker, *A Linguistic Key to the Greek New Testament*, ed. Cleon L. Rogers, Jr. (Grand Rapids, Mich.: Zondervan Publishing House, Regency Reference Library, 1980), p. 166.

This Passover celebration is the perfect opportunity to fire loaded questions at Him. With the camera lights of national attention shining in His eyes, maybe He'll slip up and say something they can use to bring Him down.

### *Silencing the Critics*

What they don't realize is that Jesus is prepared to fire back.

1. *When His authority was questioned.* Luke records the first volley in 20:2–4.

> And they spoke, saying to Him, "Tell us by what authority You are doing these things, or who is the one who gave You this authority?" And He answered and said to them, "I shall also ask you a question, and you tell Me: Was the baptism of John from heaven or from men?"

Why doesn't Jesus simply answer their question? Because He knows they've set Him up for a catch-22. On the one hand, if He says He has no earthly authority but Himself—no rabbinical school degree, no synagogue sponsorship—He discredits Himself. On the other hand, if He says His authority comes from the Lord, they could drag Him before the Romans as an insurrectionist, because the only lord the Roman government recognized was Caesar.

Shrewdly sidestepping their trap, Jesus uses their own strategy against them. If they said John's authority came from heaven, they would be forced to accept Jesus as the Messiah, because that's who John proclaimed Him to be. So now the dilemma teeters on their shoulders.

> And they reasoned among themselves, saying, "If we say, 'From heaven,' He will say, 'Why did you not believe him?' But if we say, 'From men,' all the people will stone us to death, for they are convinced that John was a prophet." And they answered that they did not know where it came from. And Jesus said to them, "Neither will I tell you by what authority I do these things." (vv. 5–8)

Score one for Jesus . . . but He's not through. With His enemies reeling, He fires another shot in the form of a well-aimed parable.

2. *When He chose to expose wrong.* Normally, Jesus' stories are difficult for the crowd to figure out. This one, however, communicates with the clarity of a lightning flash.

> And He began to tell the people this parable: "A man planted a vineyard and rented it out to vine-growers, and went on a journey for a long time. And at the harvest time he sent a slave to the vine-growers, in order that they might give him some of the produce of the vineyard; but the vine-growers beat him and sent him away empty-handed. And he proceeded to send another slave; and they beat him also and treated him shamefully, and sent him away empty-handed. And he proceeded to send a third; and this one also they wounded and cast out. And the owner of the vineyard said, 'What shall I do? I will send my beloved son; perhaps they will respect him.' But when the vine-growers saw him, they reasoned with one another, saying, 'This is the heir; let us kill him that the inheritance may be ours.' And they threw him out of the vineyard and killed him. What, therefore, will the owner of the vineyard do to them? He will come and destroy these vine-growers and will give the vineyard to others." (vv. 9–16a)

The vineyard represents the people of Israel (see Isa. 5:1–7). The owner is God, who has left His people in the hands of the vine-growers—the religious leaders. The mistreated servants sent to collect a share of the produce represent Israel's prophets. The owner's son, of course, is Jesus.[4]

Just as greed for the inheritance drives the vine-growers to murder the son, lust for power will drive the Jewish leaders to kill Jesus. Their treachery will force God to destroy them and transfer His spiritual blessing to others, the Gentiles.

Did the listeners understand the implications of Jesus' story? Their shocked response says definitely yes.

> And when they heard it, they said, "May it never be!" But He looked at them and said, "What then is this that is written,
>
> 'The stone which the builders rejected,
> This became the chief corner stone'?[5]

4. By implying that He is God's Son, Jesus subtly provides the answer to the religious leaders' previous question about His authority.

5. See Psalm 118:22. This is called a messianic psalm, because it foretells of the Messiah.

> Everyone who falls on that stone will be broken to pieces; but on whomever it falls, it will scatter him like dust." (Luke 20:16b–18)

Amazingly, these same people who cried, "May it never be!" will legislate their own disaster when they cry, "Crucify Him!"

Two lessons emerge from this parable: (1) God will vindicate His Son; the rejected stone will become "the chief corner stone." And (2) those who oppose God's plan will suffer the consequences; God will win in the end.

3. *When He was being set up.* Jesus' words should drive the religious leaders to repentance. They recognize that the parable is against them (v. 19b). But it is as if Jesus is firing into a beehive; they grow madder and madder with each hit. They attempt to grab Him right then, but fear of the people causes them to back away (v. 19a). So they regroup to formulate a more devious plan.

> And they watched Him, and sent spies who pretended to be righteous, in order that they might catch Him in some statement, so as to deliver Him up to the rule and the authority of the governor. And they questioned Him, saying, "Teacher, we know that You speak and teach correctly, and You are not partial to any, but teach the way of God in truth. Is it lawful for us to pay taxes to Caesar, or not?" (vv. 20–22)

Another catch-22. If He answers no, they will lock Him in irons and send Him to the Romans as a lawbreaker. If yes, they get the leverage they need to divide Him from His anti-tax followers. Jesus, however,

> detected their trickery and said to them, "Show Me a denarius. Whose likeness and inscription does it have?" And they said, "Caesar's." And He said to them, "Then render to Caesar the things that are Caesar's, and to God the things that are God's." (vv. 23–25)

Jesus scores again! He solves the riddle by teaching the principle that the government's authority comes from God, so we should respect it (see Prov. 8:15; Rom. 13:1–7).

How effective is Jesus' counterstrategy?

> And they were unable to catch Him in a saying in

> the presence of the people; and marveling at His answer, they became silent. (Luke 20:26)

## The Next Time You Need to Be Assertive

The lesson we learn from Jesus' encounter with the religious leaders is that it's OK to stand for what's right. It's OK to clearly proclaim the truth when God's enemies are spreading lies. We can be assertive about what we believe and not violate Christ's teaching on turning the other cheek. However, we need to stay balanced by keeping in mind the following two principles.

First, *be certain that the issue is worth a fight*. For some people, every issue is a fight. But standing up to His enemies was only a small part of Jesus' ministry. Sometimes He was content to remain silent. So we, too, need to choose our battles wisely.

Second, *be mature with the way you express yourself*. Watch your words and your tone of voice. Jesus confronted His enemies with the truth to help them see themselves for who they were. He never slandered people; neither did He bad-mouth the government.

To follow Jesus' example, we must learn to hold truth and grace in balance, to stand against sin while holding out a hand of welcome to the sinner.

## *Living Insights* STUDY ONE

Enemies come in many shapes and sizes. We may not have to match wits with a Professor Moriarty like Sherlock Holmes did, but we may have to handle a coworker who makes us look bad in front of the boss. Or a relative who tears us down emotionally. Or a neighbor who slanders us to others.

An enemy can be anyone who deliberately seeks to hurt us. How should we respond to such people? Should we stand up to them or turn the other cheek? The following questions can help us decide.

- *Is the issue worth it?* Is this a minor offense I can forgive and let go? Or is something deeper at stake? Try to pinpoint the real issue.
- *What is best for the other person?* Jesus commands us to love our enemies. Confrontation can be a powerful form of love. Is it time to let an enemy know how much his or her actions are hurting me and others?

- *Is my motive revenge?* Jesus stood up to His enemies, but He never traded insult for insult, lie for lie, hurt for hurt. Am I trying to defend myself, or strike back?

If you are struggling with a person who actively works toward your harm, ponder these questions . . . and think about one more: How can I honor Christ and uphold His name in this? That, perhaps more than anything else, will help you keep the balance between truth and grace.

## *Living Insights* — STUDY TWO

Some of us seem to be born with an irrepressible urge to express our opinions. The editorial page used to be our only public outlet. Now we can dial a radio talk show. Post a complaint on a computer bulletin board. Record our voices on a congressman's answering machine.

With all this freedom comes a great opportunity for Christians to express God's views on the issues. But with the opportunity comes an even greater responsibility to express His truth with a godly attitude. "It is unfortunate," writes Warren Wiersbe,

> that some Christians have the mistaken idea that the more obnoxious they are as citizens, the more they please God and witness for Christ. We must never violate our conscience, but we should seek to be peacemakers and not troublemakers.[6]

Consider a recent situation in which you expressed an opinion about the government, the church, or a social issue. Did your attitude and tone of voice create more light or heat?

________________________________________________

________________________________________________

________________________________________________

________________________________________________

6. Warren W. Wiersbe, *The Bible Exposition Commentary* (Wheaton, Ill.: Scripture Press Publications, Victor Books, 1989), vol. 1, p. 258.

How do you think you can state the truth without inciting arguments? What insights do you gain from Jesus' model in Luke 20?

____________________________________________

____________________________________________

____________________________________________

____________________________________________

____________________________________________

The next time you express your opinion, step back and listen to yourself. What's your tone? Are you more concerned about winning the person or the argument?

Chapter 10

# His Best . . . for Our Good

*Luke 20:27–47*

The pressure is mounting.

Huge Passover crowds surge into the city, their conversations charged with stories of Jesus' courageous cleansing of the temple and His exposure of the religious leaders' greed. The chief priests and scribes speak of Him too, but in low, rumbling, turbulent tones. Still smarting at their humiliation and threatened loss of power, they meet in dimly lit rooms behind closed doors to plot His murder.

This will be the last week of Jesus' life. A terrible storm is brewing, and when it finally breaks, the Man of Galilee will become the Man of Agony.

## Understanding the Events, Historically

All of Luke's gospel has been building toward these climactic final moments in Jesus' life. The first four chapters gave a wide-angle shot of Jesus' life, spanning His first thirty years. In the middle sixteen chapters, covering about three years, Luke presented a series of snapshots of Jesus' ministry and march to Jerusalem. In the last four chapters, he zooms in to reveal the details of Jesus' final days in dramatic close-ups.[1] And as chapter 20 comes to an end, he's turning the pages of the photo album slowly, allowing us to linger over the enlargements so as not to miss a single element of the heartrending events they record. It is in these final photos that we see the reason for the rest of Luke's book. The plot of the story is about to take a terrible twist, but it's one the main character is ready for. In fact, it's a role He's been preparing to play since the beginning of time.

## Addressing the Issues, Doctrinally

As we saw in our last study, the religious leaders have been lobbing loaded questions at Jesus. He, however, has calmly disarmed each issue with divine truth.

1. In these four chapters, Luke uses 218 verses, or a little over one-fifth of his gospel, to cover just a few days.

This is Jesus at His best—His perceptiveness and authority really shine through, particularly considering the difficulty of the hour. Let's watch Him handle another group of enemies, the Sadducees, as they pull the pin on an explosive question of their own.

This is the first and only time Luke mentions this group, so we need to take a moment to compare them with the Pharisees—a sect we're well acquainted with. Commentator William Barclay provides us the information for the following chart.[2]

| *Pharisees* | *Saddusees* |
|---|---|
| Believed the Scriptures plus the thousand rules and regulations of oral and ceremonial law. | Believed only the written Old Testament, especially the teachings of Moses, but not the prophetic books. |
| Believed in the supernatural—angels, spirits—and the resurrection of the dead. | Did not believe in the resurrection of the dead or in angels or spirits. |
| Believed in fate: all things are determined by divine decree. | Firmly held to the free will of humankind. |

As you can imagine, sparks flew whenever Pharisees and Sadducees got together. But in their mutual hatred for Christ, they found plenty of snuggle room. The Sadducees, too, devised questions to bring Jesus down, like the question in Luke 20 about the resurrection of the dead.

### *Remarriage and Resurrection*

> Now there came to Him some of the Sadducees (who say that there is no resurrection), and they questioned Him, saying, "Teacher, Moses wrote for us that if a man's brother dies, having a wife, and he is childless, his brother should take the wife and raise up offspring to his brother. Now there were seven brothers; and the first took a wife, and died childless; and the second and the third took her; and in the same way all seven died, leaving no children. Finally the woman died also. In the resurrection therefore, which one's wife will she be? For all seven had her as wife." (Luke 20:27–33)

2. William Barclay, *The Gospel of Luke*, rev. ed., The Daily Study Bible Series (Philadelphia, Pa.: Westminster Press, 1975), p. 250.

What a question! It's the kind people use to stroke a pet point, not find an answer. What are the Sadducees trying to prove? That the resurrection of the dead is a ridiculous idea, and that Jesus is wrong to teach it.[3]

We can imagine the grins on these Cheshire cats as they pose their favorite riddle. They've probably tangled many a Pharisee in this net, and Jesus would just be one more victim. Jesus, however, deftly sidesteps their hypothetical dilemma, brushing aside the incidentals and focusing on the essentials. His answer goes straight to the heart of four essential truths about the afterlife.

> And Jesus said to them, "The sons of this age marry and are given in marriage, but those who are considered worthy to attain to that age and the resurrection from the dead, neither marry, nor are given in marriage; for neither can they die anymore, for they are like angels, and are sons of God, being sons of the resurrection. But that the dead are raised, even Moses showed, in the passage about the burning bush, where he calls the Lord the God of Abraham, and the God of Isaac, and the God of Jacob. Now He is not the God of the dead, but of the living; for all live to Him." (vv. 34–38)

The first truth is this: *There is a difference between this age and the next.* We cannot view eternity through the lens of our earthly experience. The Sadducees assume that people will marry in heaven because they do on earth. Not so, according to Jesus. Their premise is wrong, so their question is irrelevant.

Second: *There will be a resurrection.* He doesn't debate this point; He simply states it (v. 35). The dead will be raised whether or not the Sadducees believe in it. Someday we all will stand before the Creator to give an account of our lives.

Third: *There will be no death beyond this life.* In heaven, the icy chill of death can't touch us, for we will be like the angels who live

3. Jesus bases much of His teaching on the doctrine of resurrection. Believers have their names written in heaven (Luke 10:20). They should not fear those who kill the body (12:4), for they will be raised from the dead to participate in the kingdom of God (13:29) and to enjoy their heavenly treasure and rewards (12:33, 42–44). Unbelievers, on the other hand, will face judgment in the hereafter (13:24–28; 16:19–31). Jesus even looks forward to His own resurrection (9:22; 18:33).

forever (v. 36; see also 1 Cor. 15:54). What will heaven be like? A veil of mystery obscures our view, but we do know that freedom from death means freedom from pain, from darkness, from deformity and disease. In heaven we will have freedom from the curse of sin.

In hell, those who reject Christ will also live forever . . . in a timeless, ever-consuming condemnation.

Fourth: *The Scriptures provide the answers*. Jesus sticks with God's Word rather than getting tied up in the Sadducees' convoluted logic. Dipping into the books of Moses—the only ones the Sadducees accept—He ladles up some meaty proof for the doctrine of resurrection. Moses himself considered the Lord to be the God of Abraham, Isaac, and Jacob—who were dead at the time. How could the Lord be their God unless their souls were alive with Him in heaven?

The Sadducees, who had approached Jesus like roaring lions, now leave in humbled silence. Only a few of the scribes dare address the Master: "Teacher, You have spoken well" (Luke 20:39). The rest of them "did not have courage to question Him any longer about anything" (v. 40).

### David and the Messiah

Jesus has affirmed more than the doctrine of resurrection. He's proven His authority and perhaps, for one brief moment, has made a dent in the leaders' hard hearts. So He seizes the opportunity to ask them a question that He hopes will penetrate the core of their beliefs.

> And He said to them, "How is it that they say the Christ is David's son? For David himself says in the book of Psalms,
>
> 'The Lord said to my Lord,
> "Sit at My right hand,
> Until I make Thine enemies a footstool for Thy feet."'
>
> David therefore calls Him 'Lord,' and how is He his son?" (vv. 41–44)

To understand Jesus' question, we have to think like a Jewish Old Testament scholar. Their studies taught them that God will rescue the Jews from their oppressors and grant the nation untold spiritual blessings through the Messiah—the anointed descendant of David. That's true, but it's only half the picture. Jesus is trying to show them that the Messiah is more than just David's son. In Psalm 110:1, David calls the Messiah "my Lord." How can David write that unless the Messiah is both human and divine—his son and the Son of God?

In terms these religious leaders can understand, Jesus reveals who He is. His authority rests not just in the fact that He is a master teacher of the Scriptures, but that He is the God of the Scriptures and the Master of creation. And if David called Him Lord, so should they.

Jesus is offering them salvation. Will they receive it?

### *Authority and Hypocrisy*

Luke doesn't mention their response, but we can assume from Jesus' next few words that it isn't favorable.

> "Beware of the scribes, who like to walk around in long robes, and love respectful greetings in the market places, and chief seats in the synagogues, and places of honor at banquets, who devour widows' houses, and for appearance's sake offer long prayers; these will receive greater condemnation." (Luke 20:46–47)

What's wrong with long robes? With being greeted respectfully? With sitting in a seat of honor? Nothing . . . unless a person *loves* those things.

Basking in the limelight that comes with their role has blinded the scribes to the reason for their religion. Pompously pious, they take advantage of the widows who support them. Their spirituality is a sham and their authority abusive; and their degradation of God's pure name and purpose will bring His wrath upon their heads in furious measure.

## Realizing the Implications, Personally

What can we gain from Jesus' example in these three scenes? Three principles that relate to the subjects of truth, salvation, and leadership.

Regarding truth: *Focus on the essentials, not the incidentals*. The Sadducees wanted to battle Jesus over useless territory. But Jesus chose to defend the more valuable ground of resurrection. We can spare ourselves a lot of needless bloodshed if we refuse to skirmish over less important issues and focus our defenses on the essential doctrines of the faith. This, in turn, will help form us into people of grace.

Regarding salvation: *Realize that Christ is the Savior, not merely the Son*. He's more than just a descendant of David or a great teacher who confronted the corrupt religious system of His day. He's Lord. And He has the power to transform our lives.

Regarding leadership: *Seek servant leadership, not the limelight*. Jesus reserved His strongest rebukes for those who used their positions of trust to further their own ends and pander to their own comforts. So we must be careful whom we follow. We need to guard against those who love places of honor, who demand respect and force their will on others. Instead, let's look for leaders who are servants of Christ and can guide us along the path of the Cross.

## *Living Insights* STUDY ONE

Have you ever won a Pyrrhic victory?

Pyrrhus was the despotic king of Epirus in the third century B.C. He won several battles against Macedonia and Rome, but his army suffered such heavy casualties that his successes were meaningless. He wore the victor's crown, but at a price greater than the benefits he sought to achieve.

When we fight over incidental issues, we run the danger of becoming like old king "win-at-all-costs" Pyrrhus. Whatever ground we gain is not worth what we lost to gain it. For instance, we may win a doctrinal argument but lose a relationship. We may triumph in a theological debate but forfeit a person's soul. That's a Pyrrhic victory.

Many church splits are such victories. So are many sibling rivalries. In-law disagreements. Divorces.

These wins taste awfully bitter, don't they? Are you battling with someone right now? How essential is the issue?

____________________________________________

____________________________________________

Is there something greater at stake? What is it?

____________________________________________

____________________________________________

What would it take to call a truce?

Remember, in Pyrrhic victories, there are no winners. Only losers. Choose your battles wisely.

## *Living Insights* STUDY TWO

The eleventh hour has struck in Jesus' life. Every tick of the clock now beats the cadence to His slow and agonizing march to the Cross. Despite the intense pressure, Jesus stays His course, continuing to preach the kingdom and stand against those who mock true religion. We marvel at His courage, His invincible strength. Indeed, this is Jesus at His best.

Standing back and watching Him put His life on the line, one wonders, *Why?* Why does He return to the temple day after day, knowingly steering Himself into this blinding gale?

Meditate on the following verses with that question in mind. Record the answers that your heart gives you.

Romans 5:7–8 ______________________________

Hebrews 9:14–15 ______________________________

1 Peter 2:23–25 ______________________________

Truly, Jesus gives His best, His all, His life . . . for our good.

Chapter 11

# LIFTING THE PROPHETIC VEIL

*Luke 21*

Death is always a surprise. We never know exactly when its shadow will fall across our door. But what if God took the surprise out of it? What if He pulled us aside and whispered the date of our death—and that date was only two months away!

How would we respond? We would probably do all we could to squeeze every ounce of life from the time we had left. And two changes would probably occur in our perspective: (1) the value of things would become more important than their cost, and (2) the eternal and intangible aspects of life would overshadow the temporal and tangible.

From the beginning, Jesus knew the date of His death. In our study of Luke, that date isn't two months away or even two weeks . . . it's about two days away.

Perhaps that's why, in Luke 21, Jesus focuses on the things death can't destroy—things like a humble, devoted heart and God's unalterable plan for the future.

## A Clarification of Two Unrelated Matters

Chapter 20 ended with Jesus warning His disciples about the scribes, who braided their piety into long, ornate prayers for people to admire, while they mercilessly robbed the most vulnerable in society (vv. 46–47).

As chapter 21 begins, Jesus looks through the mix of worshipers crisscrossing the temple, and spots an example of genuine spirituality.

### *Financial Offerings of the Rich and the Poor*

> And He looked up and saw the rich putting their gifts into the treasury. And He saw a certain poor widow putting in two small copper coins. And He said, "Truly I say to you, this poor widow put in more than all of them." (Luke 21:1–3)

How can two copper coins, which amount to less than a penny, be worth more than the gifts of the rich? Because Christ sees the value of our giving not in the amount of our money but in the devotion and sacrifice of our hearts. Although the wealthy worshipers made the offering plate clatter impressively, the *clink clink* of the widow's coins rang like silver bells in heaven,

> "for they all out of their surplus put into the offering; but she out of her poverty put in all that she had to live on." (v. 4)

With the end so near, Jesus wants His disciples to recognize what's truly valuable, which will help prepare them for the future.

The Shepherd must soon leave, and the sheep will be scattered. What can He say that will help them through the difficult days ahead?

### *Prophetic Revelations of the Near and the Far*

In verses 5–38, Jesus opens the prophetic scroll and reveals a glimmer of the near future—Jerusalem's destruction by Rome; and of the distant future—when He will come in glory.

## A Description of Things to Come

As we study Jesus' prophecy, it will be helpful to remember that sometimes when Jesus says, "The days will come," from today's perspective those days have already come and gone. Jerusalem fell, in fact, soon after the completion of the book of Acts. So, with that in mind, let's join Jesus now, as He and His disciples begin to talk as they leave the temple (see Matt. 24:1; Mark 13:1).

### *Discussion Leading to the Revelation*

The disciples "were talking about the temple, that it was adorned with beautiful stones and votive gifts" (Luke 21:5). The temple rested on Mount Zion like a glistening diamond in settings of gold. Yet, as we learned from the widow earlier, the things that dazzle people don't always impress God. Spiritual flaws fractured the foundation of the nation's worship, and in verse 6, Jesus pronounces God's judgment on this monument to man's glory:

> "As for these things which you are looking at, the days will come in which there will not be left one stone upon another which will not be torn down."

This is the up-close event in Jesus' prophecy—the fall of Jerusalem that would occur about forty years later in A.D. 70. The disciples, though, regarded the destruction of the temple and Jerusalem as the end of the world. Feeling panicky, they ask Jesus,

> "Teacher, when therefore will these things be? And what will be the sign when these things are about to take place?" (v. 7)

### *Explanations and Exhortations in the Revelation*

Without naming the exact dates, Jesus reveals the signs of the end of Jerusalem as well as the end of the world. He begins in verses 8–9 by warning of some misleading signs that could cause the disciples to jump to the wrong conclusion—that the coming of God's kingdom is closer than it truly is.

He first cautions His followers to not be misled by religious leaders who

> "come in My name, saying, 'I am He,' and, 'The time is at hand'; do not go after them." (v. 8)

When Christ returns, there will be no mistaking His arrival (compare 17:23–24).

His second warning concerns political upheavals and military strife:

> "And when you hear of wars and disturbances, do not be terrified; for these things must take place first, but the end does not follow immediately." (21:9)

This violent turmoil is only one step along the way to Christ's return, a smaller-scale version of what's to come.

With His warnings concluded, Jesus next elaborates on the kind of world disorder we can all expect before the end.

> Then He continued by saying to them, "Nation will rise against nation, and kingdom against kingdom, and there will be great earthquakes, and in various places plagues and famines; and there will be terrors and great signs from heaven." (vv. 10–11)

Here Jesus speaks of the world's end; in verse 12, however, He shifts back to the more immediate future His disciples would face.

> "But before all these things, they will lay their hands on you and will persecute you, delivering you to the synagogues and prisons, bringing you before kings and governors for My name's sake. It will lead to an

> opportunity for your testimony. So make up your minds not to prepare beforehand to defend yourselves; for I will give you utterance and wisdom which none of your opponents will be able to resist or refute. But you will be delivered up even by parents and brothers and relatives and friends, and they will put some of you to death, and you will be hated by all on account of My name." (vv. 12–17)

These verses read like a summary of the book of Acts, which chronicles the bloody trail of the men and women who carried the gospel to the ends of the earth. That trail, however, didn't end with the close of Acts and the subsequent fall of Jerusalem. It continues today in the lives of persecuted saints all over the world and will continue its rugged course until Christ returns.

Jesus ends this section by soothing our fears with this promise of eternal life: "But not a hair of your head shall perish. By your steadfast and patient endurance you shall win the true life of your souls" (vv. 18–19 AMPLIFIED). What an encouragement to hold fast to our faith!

The contrasting word *but* at the beginning of verse 20 launches a discussion of the coming judgment and desolation of Jerusalem.

> "But when you see Jerusalem surrounded by armies, then recognize that her desolation is at hand. Then let those who are in Judea flee to the mountains, and let those who are in the midst of the city depart, and let not those who are in the country enter the city; because these are days of vengeance, in order that all things which are written may be fulfilled. Woe to those who are with child and to those who nurse babes in those days; for there will be great distress upon the land, and wrath to this people, and they will fall by the edge of the sword, and will be led captive into all the nations; and Jerusalem will be trampled under foot by the Gentiles until the times of the Gentiles be fulfilled." (vv. 20–24)

In A.D. 70, Jesus' tragic prophecy was fulfilled when the Roman emperor Vespasian sent his son Titus to crush a Jewish rebellion and destroy Jerusalem. He besieged the city for five months, beginning in April when Jerusalem was filled with Passover pilgrims. The starving inhabitants were reduced to cannibalism to survive. Eventually, the Roman army breached the walls, slaughtered men, women, and children, razed the city, and demolished the temple. According to Josephus, over a million Jews perished in the war, and 97,000 were taken as slaves.[1]

Jerusalem, their beloved city, would continue to be trampled "until the times of the Gentiles be fulfilled." The "times of the Gentiles" refers to the present period, in which the Jews are experiencing, as Paul says, "a partial hardening" (Rom. 11:25). This period of time provides a window of opportunity for Gentiles to receive the Savior whom the Jews rejected. Once this time is "fulfilled," great signs will appear signaling the dawn of a new day of salvation for the Jewish nation (see Rom. 11:11–32).[2]

> "And there will be signs in sun and moon and stars, and upon the earth dismay among nations, in perplexity at the roaring of the sea and the waves, men fainting from fear and the expectation of the things which are coming upon the world; for the powers of the heavens will be shaken." (Luke 21:25–26)

Unlike the sporadic contractions of false labor, the unyielding and intensifying waves of pain throughout creation will mark the end of time. Nature will writhe and convulse until a new kingdom is born, when the Son of Man comes "with power and great glory" (v. 27; see also 2 Pet. 3:9–13).[3]

These signs also mark the end of God's judgment of the Jews that began with Jerusalem's desolation. For Jesus tells them,

> "When these things begin to take place, straighten up and lift up your heads, because your redemption is drawing near." (Luke 20:28)

The barrenness of winter is over. Like spring leaves budding on

1. See William Hendriksen, *Exposition of the Gospel according to Luke* (Grand Rapids, Mich.: Baker Book House, 1978), pp. 938–39; and William Barclay, *The Gospel of Luke*, rev. ed., The Daily Study Bible Series (Philadelphia, Pa.: Westminster Press, 1975), p. 258.

2. See David Gooding, *According to Luke: A New Exposition of the Third Gospel* (Leicester, England: InterVarsity Press; Grand Rapids, Mich.: William B. Eerdmans Publishing Co., 1987), p. 328.

3. Jesus shows us only a broad-brush mural of the end times. Other New Testament writers will later add more specific information about the Rapture of the church, the Tribulation, and the millennial kingdom.

trees, these events signal the beginning of a fruitful summer; they forecast the good news that "the kingdom of God is near" (vv. 29–31). And Jesus underlines this word of hope with a promise:

> "Truly I say to you, this generation will not pass away until all things take place.[4] Heaven and earth will pass away, but My words will not pass away." (vv. 32–33)

### A Quick Summary of Jesus' Prophecy

The path of prophecy is certainly not a smooth one, is it? Let's try to straighten out some of the twists and turns by grouping the verses according to their time frame.

| *Fall of Jerusalem* | *The "End"* |
|---|---|
| Verses 5–6: Tearing down of the temple | Verses 8–9: Misleading signs |
| Verses 12–19: Foreshadowing of the persecution Luke will record in Acts, as well as the persecution believers suffer today | Verses 10–11: Nation against nation, earthquakes, plagues, famine, terrors, and signs |
| Verses 20–24: Desolation of Jerusalem in A.D. 70 | Verses 25–28: "The Son of Man coming in . . . great glory" |
| | Verses 29–33: As the fig tree puts forth leaves, so the kingdom's coming will put forth signs |
| | Verses 34–36: "Be on guard . . . keep on the alert" |

### A Brief Reminder of Jesus' Humanity

Since Jesus gives us some strong applications in verses 34–36, let's save those for last and look ahead to verses 37–38. Here Luke takes a moment to describe Jesus' routine during His final week: teach all day in the temple, retire in the evening to the Mount of

4. Jesus isn't saying that the end will occur within the current generation. He could mean that it will occur within the generation of those who see the signs. Or, since *generation* in Greek can also be translated "race," He could be reassuring the Jews that, although God will judge them as a nation, He will not destroy them as a people. They will someday enter the kingdom.

Olives, and return early the next morning to a crowd of eager listeners. This is a touching reminder of Jesus' humanity. He is the Redeemer who will come in the clouds, but He is also the Man who feels the press of the crowds, the need for rest, and the hunger for truth.

## A Conclusion for All of Us to Remember

Like the disciples, most of us want to know when the end will come. We listen to speakers who thread prophecy into world events as easily as a string through beads. We read of wars and cataclysms in the newspaper, and we tremble as we wonder, *Could these be the signs that Jesus mentioned?*

Yet we also remember that Jesus told us to be wary of date-setters and not to be terrified. What, then, should we do while we wait? Jesus answers that question in verses 34 through 36.

First, *be on guard, resisting the things that deny His return*. These would be "dissipation and drunkenness and the worries of life" (v. 34). Our lifestyles reveal whether we truly believe Christ will return or whether we deny that He will reign as King of Kings.

Second, *keep on the alert, anticipating the One who will return*. Jesus isn't going to whisper in our ears that He's coming back in two months; He could come back any time. So we must get ready by praying for strength (v. 36) and staying ready so that we, too, can lift up our heads as our redemption draws near (v. 28).

## *Living Insights* STUDY ONE

Every day, we pick up worries and toss them into our hearts like pebbles in a burlap sack. The bills are higher than we expected—we throw in some pebbles. The house is showing signs of wear—we pitch in a few more. Another gray hair? More pebbles. Pretty soon, the sack is almost too heavy to lift. Our hearts drag the floor. And people start wondering if the scowl on our face is a permanent fixture.

Where's the joy we once had? Buried under a pile of worries.

Jesus commands us to guard against adding weights to our hearts (Luke 21:34). But how? Try this idea. Whenever you pick up a worry, before you toss it into your heart, ask yourself this question: *Would this matter if Jesus came back today?* If not, it's not worth worrying about.

OK, let's practice. Think of something you typically worry about. It may be money for a new car or needing to lose ten pounds or how clean your house is. Write it down.

______________________________________________________________

______________________________________________________________

Would this matter if Jesus came back today?

______________________________________________________________

______________________________________________________________

Of course, we shouldn't neglect responsible money management, health care, or home life because we think the Lord will return today. But we can stop *worrying* about them.

Now, on the flip side, what would matter if Jesus came back today? Probably saving a soul, healing a heart, and making sure our spiritual house is clean. What specifically would matter to you?

______________________________________________________________

______________________________________________________________

______________________________________________________________

______________________________________________________________

We can keep these burdens, not as worries, but as heartfelt concerns. And always as matters of prayer.

## *Living Insights* — STUDY TWO

Fire! The alarm screams, jolting the firehouse into action. As the firefighters scramble, blankets fly off those catching some shut-eye. A half-eaten candy bar drops on the table. A newspaper flutters to the ground.

And then . . . confusion.

"Has anyone seen my boots?" "The strap is missing on my hat. I can't wear this!" "Does anybody know where Elm Street is? I can't find the map." "All right, who took my boots?" "I think this hose has a hole in it." "Uh-oh, I forgot to fill the truck with gas." "Where are my boots!"

Can you imagine firefighters so unprepared? Of course not. Because when they're not putting out fires, they're getting ready to put out fires. They test their equipment, train for special situations, tone up their bodies to meet the rigors of the job. Only when they finish all their preparations do they rest. And even then, as long as they're on the job, they're on the alert. Because at any moment the alarm may ring.

Similarly, at any moment Christ may come again. How well are you keeping on the alert?

Jesus' prophecy tells us to expect things to get worse for Christians before they get better. When was the last time your commitment to the Lord was tested? How well-trained are you in God's Word? Is your spiritual life a little out of shape?

Firefighters aren't on the alert unless they are fully prepared. What do you need to do to better prepare for Christ's return?

________________________________________

________________________________________

________________________________________

It's been about two thousand years since Christ promised He would return, and we're still waiting for His alarm. It may be another two thousand years before it rings, but, then again, this could be the day. Are you ready?

Chapter 12

# STRONG LEADERSHIP IN STORMY TIMES

*Luke 22:1–30*

Like an epic tale rife with tragedy, courage, and noble triumph, so reads Luke's account of Jesus' last two days. Each scene resonates with the best and worst of good and evil: the deception of the traitor . . . the Last Supper . . . the agony of Gethsemane . . . the arrest by a mob . . . the denial of Peter . . . torture and trials . . . Golgotha.

Two thousand years of history, however, can diminish the impact of its most shattering event—the crucifixion of God's innocent Son, Jesus Christ. With the filter of time, the blood-red brutality of the corrupt chief priests, scribes, and elders can pale to safely gilded illustrations in worn, old Bibles, harmless and remote.

Unless we take the time to put ourselves there. Unless we stop to live through, in our hearts and minds, what Jesus lived through in reality.

Only when we come alongside Him can we feel the terror, danger, and deep evil He faces as Satan stalks Him on the way to the Cross. And only then can we see the resolute leadership, determination, and greatheartedness of Christ, the Conqueror.

## The Gathering Storm

As Jesus plans to quietly celebrate the Passover with His disciples, storm clouds of betrayal gather on the horizon.

### *The Time*

> Now the Feast of Unleavened Bread, which is called the Passover, was approaching. (Luke 22:1)

The Feast of Unleavened Bread lasts an entire week and begins with the Passover meal. This meal commemorates the deliverance of the ancient Hebrews from Egyptian slavery and from death, when the Lord passed over the homes whose doorposts had been smeared with the blood of a lamb (see Exod. 12). It was "a permanent ordinance," a memorial to be celebrated throughout all generations (v. 14).

So thousands of Jews from all over the world crowd into Jerusalem to sacrifice their Passover lambs in the temple. For many, this fulfills a lifelong dream. They come to bask in the temple's purifying light. To hear songs of praise sung in a dozen languages. To smell the smoke from their sacrifices as it curls up to God. To sip the cup of freedom with their fellow Jews. To pray that, maybe this year, God will reveal the final Moses—the Messiah.

These are the devoted worshipers whose hearts Jesus has stirred in the temple. They are also the multitude the religious leaders fear.

### *The People*

Magnetized by their mutual hatred for Jesus, the opposite poles of the chief priests and scribes seek "how they might put Him to death" (Luke 22:2). Jesus is a loose dagger that might cut their purse strings and their power. To make matters worse, He's dangerously popular. How can they get at Him away from the crowds? They need someone on the inside.

### *The Plan*

> And Satan entered into Judas who was called Iscariot, belonging to the number of the twelve. And he went away and discussed with the chief priests and officers how he might betray Him to them. And they were glad, and agreed to give him money. And he consented, and began seeking a good opportunity to betray Him to them apart from the multitude. (vv. 3–6)

From the heights of Christ's companionship Judas plunges to hell itself, becoming a servant of Satan. His own heart and soul, though, are what he's really bartered away to the religious leaders.

## The Memorable Meal

With the betrayer in position, the chief priests and scribes now wait, poised to strike. Yet Jesus is fully aware of their plans, knowing that God will use their wickedness to accomplish His mission.

> Then came the first day of Unleavened Bread on which the Passover lamb had to be sacrificed. And He sent Peter and John, saying, "Go and prepare the Passover for us, that we may eat it." And

they said to Him, "Where do You want us to prepare it?" (vv. 7–9)

Because of the Passover crowds, there's not an open room within miles of Jerusalem. Jesus, however, has matters in hand. He tells Peter and John that, once they enter the city, they will find a man carrying a pitcher of water—a task women usually perform, so he will be easy to spot. This man will lead them to a house that has an upper room, furnished and available (vv. 10–12). Finding "everything just as He had told them," Peter and John sacrifice the lamb in the temple and prepare the Passover (v. 13).

### *Reclining at the Table*

Reclining at the low U-shaped table, they eat while lying on pillows, leaning on their left elbows and with their feet away from the table.

In the flickering light from the oil lamps, they look on the ancient symbols of Israel's deliverance: roasted lamb, the sacrifice that saved their lives; flat, round pieces of unleavened bread, a reminder of their urgent haste; bitter herbs, reminiscent of their bitter slavery; salt water, symbolizing their tears; and *charoseth*, a savory chutney made of apples and nuts, which calls to mind the mixture they used for making bricks.[1]

The traditional Passover meal followed a long-standing tradition of events:

> 1. A prayer of thanksgiving by the head of the house; drinking the first cup of (diluted) wine.
> 2. The eating of bitter herbs. . . .
> 3. The son's inquiry, "Why is this night distinguished from all other nights?" and the father's appropriate reply, either narrated or read.
> 4. The singing of the first part of the Hallel (Psalms 113, 114), and the washing of hands. The second cup.
> 5. The carving and eating of the lamb, together with unleavened bread. . . .
> 6. Continuation of the meal, each eating as

1. See Ralph Gower, *The New Manners and Customs of Bible Times* (Chicago, Ill.: Moody Press, 1987), p. 357; and Ceil and Moishe Rosen, *Christ in the Passover* (Chicago, Ill.: Moody Press, 1978), pp. 51, 68–69.

much as he liked, but always last of the lamb. The third cup.

7. Singing of the last part of the Hallel (Psalms 115–118). Fourth cup.[2]

Little do the disciples realize that the fulfillment of all their symbols and traditions reclines in their midst. John, on His right, leans back on Jesus' breast to ask a question (see John 13:25). Judas, on Jesus' left, will receive the bread and bitter herbs from Jesus' own hand (see v. 26). Reclining as they are, Judas occupies the seat of highest honor and trust—at Jesus' back. To the very end, Jesus lovingly appeals to Judas to change His mind, both with the position of honor and the morsel of food.

As the Passover begins, Jesus lifts a cup of wine, looks into the eyes of His disciples, and says,

> "I have earnestly desired to eat this Passover with you before I suffer; for I say to you, I shall never again eat it until it is fulfilled in the kingdom of God." And when He had taken a cup and given thanks, He said, "Take this and share it among yourselves; for I say to you, I will not drink of the fruit of the vine from now on until the kingdom of God comes." (Luke 22:15–18)

The disciples have no idea what Jesus means by *suffer*. He has tried to forewarn them, but there's no place for a dead king in their visions of the kingdom. So they hear what they want to hear and discard what doesn't fit.

Realizing that time is slipping away, Jesus keeps trying to break through to them. He offers His men bite-sized words and images they can digest and remember.

Taking a piece of unleavened bread, He gives thanks, breaks it, offers it to them, and says, "This is My body which is given for you; do this in remembrance of Me" (v. 19).

After the meal, He takes another cup of wine, probably the third cup in the Passover ceremony,[3] and says, "This cup which is

2. William Hendriksen, *Exposition of the Gospel according to Luke* (Grand Rapids, Mich.: Baker Book House, 1978), pp. 959–60.

3. "The Mishnah states that the third cup was the most significant of all. [It] had two names: the 'cup of blessing,' because it came after the blessing or grace after meals, and the 'cup of redemption,' because it represented the blood of the Paschal lamb." Ceil and Moishe Rosen, *Christ in the Passover*, p. 59.

poured out for you is the new covenant in My blood" (v. 20). Under the old covenant, the blood of animals temporarily atoned for sin. Now Jesus establishes a new and better covenant. As both High Priest and Passover Lamb, He offers His own blood as an atonement, obtaining for us a permanent eternal redemption (see Heb. 9:1–7, 11–15, 23–28).

### *Revealing the Plot*

Suffering? Blood? *New* covenant? The disciples struggle to comprehend. But then Jesus discloses something that really sets their minds reeling.

> "But behold, the hand of the one betraying Me is with Me on the table. For indeed, the Son of Man is going as it has been determined; but woe to that man by whom He is betrayed!" And they began to discuss among themselves which one of them it might be who was going to do this thing. (Luke 22: 21–23)

According to Mark's account, Jesus' words grieve them, and they "say to Him one by one, 'Surely not I?'" (Mark 14:19). They never guessed it would be Judas (see John 13:29). So they glance furtively at one another. Eyebrows raise. Fingers point. Innuendos fly.

## The Childish Dispute

From this churning pot of suspicion, pride rises to the surface.

### *Disciples' Argument*

> And there arose also a dispute among them as to which one of them was regarded to be greatest. (Luke 22:24)

We can almost hear them bickering like children on the playground. "Betray Jesus? I'd take fifty lashes, and I still wouldn't betray Him." "I'd take a hundred!" "Oh yeah? Well, I'd . . . I'd take a thousand!"

How sad that, on the eve of the Crucifixion, Jesus' closest followers comprehend so little of His heart. They need a lesson on humility that they will never forget.

### *Jesus' Answer*

> And He said to them, "The kings of the Gentiles

> lord it over them; and those who have authority over them are called 'Benefactors.' But not so with you, but let him who is the greatest among you become as the youngest, and the leader as the servant." (vv. 25–26)

Probably at this point Jesus rises from the table, takes off His outer garment, wraps a towel around His waist, and begins washing the disciples' feet (see John 13:1–15). After He takes off the towel, Jesus reviews the lesson:

> "For who is greater, the one who reclines at the table, or the one who serves? Is it not the one who reclines at the table? But I am among you as the one who serves." (Luke 22:27)

The implication is this: if we want to model Him, we'll become servants too. There's no pulling rank in His army. No preoccupation with titles. No emphasis on protocol and special privileges. This is what it will be like to live in the kingdom that Jesus promises:

> "And you are those who have stood by Me in My trials; and just as My Father has granted Me a kingdom, I grant you that you may eat and drink at My table in My kingdom, and you will sit on thrones judging the twelve tribes of Israel." (vv. 28–30)

## The Lasting Lesson

We have eaten the bitter herbs of Israel's suffering and heard Jesus say that He must suffer too. We have eaten the sacrificial lamb, while across the table sits the Lamb of God. We have taken the broken bread from Him whose body was broken for us. We have received the cup from the One whose blood was poured out for our redemption. We have seen our Master put on a servant's towel and felt the water of forgiveness wash us clean.

All who enter the Upper Room leave with a sense of awe. Jesus is our strong-hearted leader. Yet it is with servant-hearted humility that He has conquered sin and Satan. Death has passed over us. And now, we are free.

## *Living Insights* STUDY ONE

Do you wonder what Jesus thought as He surveyed the Passover table?

Perhaps seeing the sacrificed lamb took Him back to His first day of ministry by the Jordan, with John's words still ringing in His ears: "Behold, the Lamb of God who takes away the sin of the world!" (John 1:29). The months that followed brought so many people to heal and hearts to touch. So many early mornings in prayer and late nights talking by the fire. So many tears to cry along the way. And now, on His final day of ministry, the Passover calls out to Him again: "Behold, the Lamb of God who takes away the sin of the world."

Surely, images of the first Passover come to mind—God's curse of death; the bleating lambs; the head of the house plunging his knife into the innocent yearling, drawing its life's blood and smearing it on the doorpost. Perhaps, at that moment, the words of Isaiah 53 plunge into His heart like never before: "He was pierced through . . . He was crushed . . . Like a lamb that is led to slaughter" (vv. 5, 7).

◆

What do you think about when you survey the communion table at your church? Based on our study of the Passover and the Last Supper, what images can you dwell on to make your communion experience more meaningful?

____________________________________________________________

____________________________________________________________

____________________________________________________________

The next time you cradle the bread and the cup in your hands, remember the day God passed over you. Remember, and give thanks.

## *Living Insights* STUDY TWO

We have heard the apostle Paul's words so often during communion that we can easily overlook them, like a few familiar books in a vast library. "The Lord Jesus in the night in which He was betrayed took bread" (1 Cor. 11:23). In *Reliving the Passion*, Walter Wangerin pulls Paul's words down from the shelf for us and unlocks their rich meaning.

> When did Jesus choose to give us the supernal, enduring gift of his presence . . . his dear communing with us? When we were worthy of the gift, good people indeed? Hardly. It was precisely when we were most unworthy. When our wickedness was directed particularly at him.
>
> . . . In the night when his people betrayed him—the night of intensest enmity—the dear Lord Jesus said, "This is my blood of the covenant, poured out for many." Then! Can we comprehend the joining of two such extremes, the good and the evil together? In the night of gravest human treachery he gave the gift of himself. And the giving has never ceased. The holy communion continues today. . . .
>
> Oh, this is a love past human expectation. This is beyond all human deserving. This, therefore, is a love so celestial that it shall endure long and longer then we do.
>
> This is grace.[4]

Have you ever felt like you've played the Judas, that you've sold out your Lord for thirty pieces of sin? He still offers you His morsel of love from the Passover table. Take it. Eat it. Receive His grace.

## *Digging Deeper*

To enter more deeply into this Passover night with Jesus, read the Hallel, Psalms 113 through 118. Hear Him singing these ancient hymns, feel what the words must have meant to Him, see how these psalms poignantly foreshadowed His life, death, resurrection, and reign.

4. Walter Wangerin, Jr., *Reliving the Passion* (Grand Rapids, Mich.: Zondervan Publishing House, 1992), pp. 54–55.

Chapter 13

# The Darkest of All Nights

*Luke 22:31–62*

While Jesus and His disciples celebrate the Passover, night falls on Jerusalem. The hectic clamor of city life settles into the rhythmic chirping of crickets. The moon's pale light pours over the temple walls into the Kidron Valley and splashes up the Mount of Olives.

In the Upper Room, oil lamps throw flickering ghosts against the walls. Satan is here, crouching in the shadows, moving his pawn into position. With a morsel of food and a searching look, Jesus gives Judas one last chance to redirect his heart. But Judas is immovable; he receives the food but refuses the offer. Breathing a sigh of sorrow, Jesus concedes, "What you do, do quickly" (John 13:27). And with those words, He sends both the pawn and his master into the night to carry out their treacherous plans.

Once outside, Judas hurries down the steps and into the street. He pulls his cloak around his neck, worried that someone might recognize him. Just to make sure, he slips down a few back alleys, padding across the cold pavement like a nervous cat. Heart pounding and out of breath, he finally arrives at the chief priest's house and raps on the door. When the door opens, Judas glances behind him one last time.

As he ducks inside, a thick, black curtain of evil descends upon the city. This will be the darkest night the world has ever known, for all the powers of darkness are converged to snuff out the Light of the World.

## Realistic Reminders

Back in the Upper Room, Jesus has a few moments to prepare His disciples for the darkness that awaits them. As it turns out, Judas isn't Satan's only target. He's aiming his sights at a bigger prize.[1]

> "Simon, Simon, behold, Satan has demanded

1. See Matthew 16:18–19 for the reason Satan singles out Peter.

> permission to sift you like wheat; but I have prayed for you, that your faith may not fail; and you, when once you have turned again, strengthen your brothers." (Luke 22:31–32)

Jesus knows the frailty of the human heart, yet He also sees in Peter a resiliency of spirit. So He encourages and supports him, but Peter denies that he needs any help at all.

> And he said to Him, "Lord, with You I am ready to go both to prison and to death!" And He said, "I say to you, Peter, the cock will not crow today until you have denied three times that you know Me." (vv. 33–34)

Peter's overconfidence reminds us of two truths about ourselves: (1) no matter how confident we may feel, we are all human, and (2) no matter how devoted we may be to Christ, we will all fail (compare 1 Cor. 10:12). Satan often attacks us where we think we're strongest, because he knows we are trusting in our own strength instead of God's.

Before dawn, Satan will crush Peter's spirit and reveal to him the layers of chaff in his life. But Jesus has prayed for him. A kernel of faith will survive. Someday, he'll use this experience to strengthen Jesus' other disciples, who will also fail their Lord on this dark and dreadful night.

## Regrettable Failures

In the following verses, Jesus warns His friends one last time of the dangers that lie ahead. He Himself is going to be "numbered with the transgressors" (Luke 22:37) and suffer in agony as Isaiah prophesied (see Isa. 53).

While He has been in the world, He has been its light. But He won't be with them much longer, for the night has come (see John 9:4–5; 12:35). So He counsels them to take their purses and bags and even arm themselves (Luke 22:35–38; compare 9:1–6), underscoring that they won't have the safety of His light when He leaves. Rather, they will have to be lights in the darkness themselves (see John 12:36; Phil. 2:15).

For that they will need more than swords; they will need a faith of tempered steel—the kind of faith Jesus wields in Gethsemane.

### *Unfaithful Disciples*

> And He came out and proceeded as was His custom[2] to the Mount of Olives; and the disciples also followed Him. And when He arrived at the place, He said to them, "Pray that you may not enter into temptation." And He withdrew from them about a stone's throw, and He knelt down and began to pray, saying, "Father, if Thou art willing, remove this cup from Me; yet not My will, but Thine be done." Now an angel from heaven appeared to Him, strengthening Him. And being in agony He was praying very fervently; and His sweat became like drops of blood, falling down upon the ground. And when He rose from prayer, He came to the disciples and found them sleeping from sorrow, and said to them, "Why are you sleeping? Rise and pray that you may not enter into temptation." (Luke 22:39–46)

The Creator of angels now needs an angel's strength. The One who changed water into the wine of joy now watches His sweat become bloody drops of agony. The perfectly obedient Son now cries out to His Father, "Remove this cup!"[3]

Isn't there any other way to redeem the world? Jesus knows the answer. So He yields Himself: "Yet not My will, but Thine be done." The real battle of the Cross was fought and won here.

Jesus needs His disciples to help bear His load. Yet even loyal Peter, who said he would fight beside Jesus to the death, can't fend off sleep long enough to pray. According to Matthew's account, Jesus has to shake his friends awake three times (Matt. 26:36–46). The disciples are already exhausted by sorrow (Luke 22:45), yet the sorrow has barely begun.

2. Commentator Michael Wilcock illuminates this phrase's significance: "As [Luke] has been revealing Satan's plan of destruction and God's plan of salvation, it has become apparent that they are *both driving towards the same object*. Jesus's enemies are bending all their efforts and their ingenuity to bring him to the cross; yet that is the very 'cup' which the Father has given him to drink. . . . Jesus has gone to the garden 'as was his custom' . . . . He has gone deliberately into a trap from which he could have escaped with ease. His enemies are carrying out their plans, but he is altogether in control." *The Message of Luke*, The Bible Speaks Today series (Downers Grove, Ill.: InterVarsity Press, 1979), p. 193.

3. Jesus did not fear the cup of suffering His enemies would give Him. At this moment, He was gazing into the cup of God's wrath (see Isa. 51:17–20).

Have you ever prayed for something with such intensity that you dropped to your knees, buried your face in the ground, and burst into tears? With every sob, your heart cried out to God, "Please, heal my child!" or "End this hardship!" or "Let me live!" You long for someone to struggle alongside you, but you're left to crawl through as Jesus did—on His knees, alone.

Jesus' most trusted friends failed to stand by Him in His most difficult hour. And so it may be for us, when it is our time to kneel in Gethsemane (compare John 15:20).

### *Deceitful Judas*

Jesus arrives on the other side of His struggle fully resigned to the Father's will, at peace, and invincible. Just in time, because at that moment a snakelike trail of torch-bearing soldiers and officials slithers into the garden. Judas is at its head, with poison in his kiss (Luke 22:47).

> But Jesus said to him, "Judas, are you betraying the Son of Man with a kiss?" And when those who were around Him saw what was going to happen, they said, "Lord, shall we strike with the sword?" And a certain one of them struck the slave of the high priest and cut off his right ear. But Jesus answered and said, "Stop! No more of this." And He touched his ear and healed him. And Jesus said to the chief priests and officers of the temple and elders who had come against Him, "Have you come out with swords and clubs as against a robber? While I was with you daily in the temple, you did not lay hands on Me; but this hour and the power of darkness are yours." (vv. 48–53)

Say the name *Judas*. You can still taste the bitter betrayal these many centuries later, can't you? How stunned the other disciples must have been. And confused. Thinking back to Jesus' earlier instructions to procure swords (vv. 36, 38), they think this must be the time to fight. Peter, impetuous as ever, even lops off the high priest's servant's ear (v. 50; see also John 18:10).

But what a picture of mercy and constancy we see in Jesus. As He has so many times before, He again brings relief and healing—even to His enemy's servant. He reattaches the slave's ear and stays the course His Father has set Him (Luke 22:51).

And He keeps on telling the truth, revealing the deadly darkness in the religious leaders' souls (v. 53; see also John 3:19–20).

***Fearful Peter***

In shock, the disciples watch the guards tie up their Lion of Judah and lead Him away like a lamb (Luke 22:54a). The mob snakes away with its prey, and the frightened disciples scatter into the night. Even Peter.

Peter takes his first downward step into denial when he decides to follow the mob to the high priest's house "at a distance" (v. 54b). He longs to be near Jesus, but fear pulls him into the shadows.

Once in the courtyard, he takes another step down by trying to blend in with the arrest party by the fire (v. 55). Perhaps he rationalizes, *I'm more help to Jesus out here than in prison*.

Having made the compromise to conceal his identity, he must now back up his actions with his words. When a servant girl recognizes him, he slips into outright denial: "Woman, I do not know Him" (vv. 56–57).

The spiraling descent rapidly lands him in the darkest pit of his sin. Another person says, "You are one of them too!" Peter retorts, "Man, I am not!" (v. 58). However, his Galilean accent betrays him, and another man says, "Certainly this man also was with Him, for he is a Galilean too." Mark tells us that Peter begins to curse and swear, "I do not know this man you are talking about!" (Mark 14:71).

"While he was still speaking"—while his desperate expletives hung in the night air—"a cock crowed," and "the Lord turned and looked at Peter" (Luke 22:60–61a).

Jesus didn't say anything. Neither did He give him an I-told-you-so smirk. He just looked at Peter. "That voiceless, grief-laden look," writes William Barclay, "went to his heart like a sword and opened a fountain of tears."[4]

> And Peter remembered the word of the Lord, how He had told him, "Before a cock crows today, you will deny Me three times." And he went out and wept bitterly. (vv. 61b–62)

4. William Barclay, *The Gospel of Luke*, rev. ed., The Daily Study Bible Series (Philadelphia, Pa.: Westminster Press, 1975), p. 270.

### *Remarkable Changes*

The light of dawn finally creeps across the city, pushing back the darkness. But it's too late; the evil work has been done. The betrayer has come out of hiding. God's Son is in the clutches of His enemies. Jesus' followers are in disarray. And Peter, the Rock of Gibraltar in the movement, lies broken in pieces.

As we prepare to follow Christ's blood-stained path to the cross, let's reflect on what took place that dark night while Jerusalem slept. We learn at least three lessons.

First, *everyone must endure a Gethsemane*. Ken Gire has written, "Gethsemane is where we go when there's no place to go but God."[5] It is a lonely place but a necessary one if we are to learn submission to the fullest extent. For only when all others have been faithless can we discover God's true faithfulness.

Second, *everyone will experience betrayal*. This is one of those bitter pills life forces us to swallow. A close friend, a trusted coworker, even our spouse may deceive us. Oh, the heartache of betrayal! But it teaches us reality, and it forces us to cling tighter to God.

Third, *everyone has exhibited failure*. As with Peter, failure is humiliating and devastating. It shoves all our inadequacies into our faces. But it also has the power to clear away the dross of our lives and produce in us the shining quality of humility.

## *Living Insights* STUDY ONE

We think of Peter as the disciple who denied Jesus, but didn't the rest, by their absence, deny Him too? Don't we all deny Him in similar ways today?

> When I am too busy to pray, I deny that you are
> the center of my life.
> When I neglect your Word, I deny that you are
> competent to guide me.
> When I worry, I deny that you are Lord of my
> circumstances.[6]

5. Ken Gire, *Intense Moments with the Savior* (Grand Rapids, Mich.: Zondervan Publishing House, 1994), p. 81.

6. Ken Gire, *Intimate Moments with the Savior* (Grand Rapids, Mich.: Zondervan Publishing House, 1989), p. 103.

Listen for a moment. Do you hear a rooster crowing an indictment that you've denied your Lord? If so, how?

We should not be too hard on Peter, and neither should we be too hard on ourselves. Jesus looks at us in our failure with the same look He gave Peter—one filled with honesty and empathy. Later, He restored the repentant disciple and gave him even greater responsibilities (see John 21). He can restore you as well.

## *Living Insights* STUDY TWO

The Gethsemane experience is a process. We enter trembling and sweating and crying out to the Lord: "Remove this cup!" Then, somewhere in the midst of our agony, the Lord touches us, and we leave in peace: "Not my will, but Thine be done" (Luke 22:42).

Sometimes, however, well-meaning sermons and books violate the process by installing a revolving gate on the garden, rushing us in and out. We get the idea that good Christians are able to respond to deep heartache with quick submission. But—listen well, Christian—our Lord first felt His pain to the fullest before He experienced peace. Should we expect anything less for ourselves?

Others, to the opposite extreme, would have us never leave the garden. We need to remember that there is life beyond our struggles, that we can accept God's cup and rest in His will.

Ella Wheeler Wilcox once wrote,

> All those who journey, soon or late,
> Must pass within the garden's gate;
> Must kneel alone in darkness there,
> And battle with some fierce despair.
> God pity those who cannot say,
> "Not mine but thine," who only pray,
> "Let this cup pass," and cannot see

The purpose in Gethsemane.[7]

To discover the deeper faith God has for us, we can't bypass our Gethsemanes. Neither can we live in them forever. We must go through.

Where are you? Are you outside the walls, afraid to enter the garden and feel your grief to its fullest? Or are you inside, afraid to say, "Not my will, but Thine be done," and leave your pain in God's hands?

Whatever your situation, remember you're not alone. Jesus entered the garden before you, and He's willing to lead you through.

7. From Ella Wheeler Wilcox's "Gethsemane," as quoted by Clarence Edward Macartney, in *Great Nights of the Bible* (New York, N.Y.: Abingdon-Cokesbury Press, 1943), p. 166.

Chapter 14

# THE DAY CHRIST DIED

*Luke 22:63–23:46*

The cross of Calvary remains the greatest paradox of all time. Consider this and wonder:

- The same injustice that condemned innocent Jesus accomplished the justice of God.
- The cruel hands that grasped the whip and wielded the mallet moved as instruments of God's holy purpose.
- The diabolical plot to murder the Son of God became the means through which the world was released from Satan's grasp.
- The cross, which symbolized fear and brutality, now shines as a beacon of hope to the world.

Jesus was crucified for all the wrong reasons—hatred, jealousy, greed. But out of this polluted soil God grew the tree of eternal life.

His death was bittersweet. Bitter as the gall He drank during His suffering and sweet as the forgiveness He offers all who believe. As we follow Jesus through His valley of death, we must not forget the grace that marks our every step.

## Jesus in Custody

After His arrest, Jesus is rushed through six shamefully unjust trials (summarized in detail in the chart at the end of this chapter). Luke records four of them, omitting the trials before Annas (see John 18:12–13, 19–23) and Caiaphas (see Matt. 26:57–68).

Annas was the ex-high priest and mafia boss who still held the reins in the temple moneymaking operation. He wanted revenge on Jesus for throwing out the money changers and disrupting "business." After questioning Him, Annas sent Jesus to his son-in-law, the current high priest, Caiaphas. His assignment: to charge Jesus with a crime punishable by death. Blasphemy would do.

After these unlawful nighttime trials, Caiaphas put Jesus into the custody of the temple officers, which is where Luke picks up the story.

Eager to exact their own pound of flesh for the troubles He's caused them, they circle Jesus like jackals around a wounded lion.

Hateful words escalate to physical violence as one of them shoves Jesus into the waiting fist of another. Jesus staggers. They all laugh. Then one man gets an idea for a cruel game; he ties a twisted rag over Jesus' eyes. "Prophesy," he shouts, shoving Him into another man's waiting punch to the stomach. "Who is the one who hit You?" (Luke 22:64). Coarse laughter erupts once more. On through the dark night, they continue beating and jeering and, ironically, "blaspheming" (v. 65).

## Jesus on Trial

The first rays of dawn finally put a stop to their sadistic sport, and they haul Jesus away for His third trial.

### *Before the Council of Elders (Sanhedrin)*

A meeting of the Council of Elders, or Sanhedrin, is necessary to officially convict Jesus. According to William Barclay, certain trial laws governed such cases.

> All charges must be supported by the evidence of two witnesses independently examined. . . . Sentence of death could never be carried out on the day on which it was given; a night must elapse so that the court might sleep on it, so that, perchance, their condemnation might turn to mercy.[1]

Mercy and proper procedure, however, are not on the court's docket this morning. Robed in self-righteousness, the rulers lick their lips as they eye their prey. Before them stands a frail figure, His face swollen and bruised from the beating. Without His multitude of followers nearby, He doesn't look so intimidating to them. It takes just a few minutes to railroad a guilty verdict.

> "If You are the Christ, tell us." But He said to them, "If I tell you, you will not believe; and if I ask a question, you will not answer. But from now on the Son of Man will be seated at the right hand of the power of God." And they all said, "Are You the Son of God, then?" And He said to them, "Yes, I am."

1. William Barclay, *The Gospel of Luke*, rev. ed., The Daily Study Bible Series (Philadelphia, Pa.: The Westminster Press, 1975), p. 276.

> And they said, "What further need do we have of testimony? For we have heard it ourselves from His own mouth."
>
> Then the whole body of them arose and brought Him before Pilate. (Luke 22:67–23:1)

### *Before Governor Pilate*

They bring Him to Pilate because only the Romans can carry out capital punishment. Figuring he will simply shrug his shoulders at their charges of blasphemy, the chief priests concoct three false accusations, hoping one of them will stick.

> And they began to accuse Him, saying, "We found this man misleading our nation and forbidding to pay taxes to Caesar, and saying that He Himself is Christ, a King." And Pilate asked Him, saying, "Are You the King of the Jews?" And He answered him and said, "It is as you say." And Pilate said to the chief priests and the multitudes, "I find no guilt in this man." But they kept on insisting, saying, "He stirs up the people, teaching all over Judea, starting from Galilee, even as far as this place." (23:2–5)

Notice that Pilate proclaims Him innocent, but he senses some dangerous undercurrents in this situation. The Jews had revolted in the past when he got in over his head concerning their religious matters. The last thing he needs is for more waves to ripple back to Rome. So, when he hears that Jesus is from Galilee, he sees a way to smooth things out for himself. He can send Jesus to Herod Antipas, the ruler of Galilee, for a verdict (vv. 6–7).

### *Before Herod Antipas*

> Now Herod was very glad when he saw Jesus; for he had wanted to see Him for a long time, because he had been hearing about Him and was hoping to see some sign performed by Him. And he questioned Him at some length; but He answered him nothing. (vv. 8–9)

Jesus refuses to become a court clown and whip up a miracle for Herod's entertainment. He says nothing, holding His words like pearls lest this pompous swine trample them underfoot.

The chief priests and scribes, however, are quick to fill the silence with accusations: "See, He's no Messiah—He's a fraud!" Herod and his soldiers join in the ridicule, "treating Him with contempt and mocking Him." To cap the farce, Herod dresses Him "in a gorgeous robe" and sends Him back to Pilate—without a verdict (vv. 10–11).

***Back before Pilate***

Once again, the gaunt silhouette of Jesus stands before Pilate. Deep in the Roman governor's heart, he knows that this man is no threat to the state. So he summons the chief priests, the rulers, and the people and declares,

> "You brought this man to me as one who incites the people to rebellion, and behold, having examined Him before you, I have found no guilt in this man regarding the charges which you make against Him. No, nor has Herod, for he sent Him back to us; and behold, nothing deserving death has been done by Him. I will therefore punish Him and release Him." (vv. 14–16)

Pilate's verdict echoes the words of the prophet, "He had done no violence, Nor was there any deceit in His mouth" (Isa. 53:9b). The Lamb of God is spotless and pure, yet—here is the paradox—"the Lord has caused the iniquity of us all To fall on Him" (v. 6b). He bears our sentence of death so that we might be set free—much like what happens at the release of Barabbas.

Pilate customarily releases one prisoner during the Passover (Luke 23:17). By this means, he hopes to set Jesus free, as well as satisfy his own conscience. But the people block his escape route, shouting, "Away with this man, and release for us Barabbas!"—a notorious outlaw, under arrest for insurrection and murder (vv. 18–19).[2]

Condemn an innocent man and let a murderer go free? It makes no sense to Pilate. "Wanting to release Jesus," Pilate addresses them again, but they are impervious to logic (v. 20). A savage chant begins to surge through the crowd: "Crucify, crucify Him!" (v. 21).

2. According to John's account, Pilate has Jesus scourged after the people cry out for Barabbas' release. Apparently, he hopes that, when they see Jesus punished so severely, they will either take pity on Him or recognize that He is no king. Pilate, however, does not calculate the crowd's frenzied thirst for Jesus' blood (see John 19:1–6).

A third time, Pilate pleads with the people. But their voices build into crashing waves, pounding him until he relents.

> And Pilate pronounced sentence that their demand should be granted. And he released the man they were asking for who had been thrown into prison for insurrection and murder, but he delivered Jesus to their will. (vv. 24–25)

## Jesus En Route to Golgotha

To add to the shame of crucifixion, the Romans would force the condemned criminal to carry the horizontal cross beam through the city to the place of execution. The weakened Jesus stumbles under the weight of the heavy beam, so a soldier presses Simon of Cyrene into carrying it for Him (v. 26).

Stringing behind Jesus on His death march is a great multitude of people. Among them are many women, "mourning and lamenting Him" (v. 27). Jesus, however, turns toward them with a heart of concern not for Himself but for the people who will one day bear the much heavier cross of God's judgment:

> "Daughters of Jerusalem, stop weeping for Me, but weep for yourselves and for your children. For behold, the days are coming when they will say, 'Blessed are the barren, and the wombs that never bore, and the breasts that never nursed.' Then they will begin to say to the mountains, 'Fall on us,' and to the hills, 'Cover us.' For if they do these things in the green tree, what will happen in the dry?" (vv. 28–31)

## Jesus at Calvary

Soon, Jesus and two other men to be crucified arrive at "the place called The Skull" (v. 33), and the soldiers begin their grisly task.

### *Soldiers and Criminals*

In his book *Rabboni*, Phillip Keller conveys the horror of crucifixion:

> Jesus was stretched out prostrate on the cross beams. . . . With the ominous sound of iron on iron, the nails pierced His sinews and flesh. Blood spurted from the wounds as the spikes sank into the

> tough wood. He writhed in pain. Then His feet were laid flat on the wood with His legs drawn up. Two more terrible spikes did their dreadful work.
>
> Like the thousands of other lambskins stretched in the midmorning sun that day, so the Son of God lay stretched beneath the burning skies of Judea. God's Passover Lamb was there for all to see. . . .
>
> . . . It was the most ghastly altar upon which any human sacrifice had ever been offered. God very God hanged there suspended between heaven and earth as the supreme substitute.[3]

### *Words and Feelings*

For six torturous hours, Jesus hangs on the cross. To breathe, He must stretch Himself upward, pushing against the spike in His feet. Every movement shoots searing pain through His body. His leg muscles cramp into fistlike knots. His shoulders dislocate from their sockets as they bear the weight of His body. His skin burns with a feverish sweat. Victims usually curse and wail, but Jesus holds His sufferings to Himself.

Only seven times does He speak. Luke records three of Jesus' statements—one to His executioners, "Father, forgive them; for they do not know what they are doing" (v. 34); one to the repentant thief, "Truly I say to you, today you shall be with Me in Paradise" (v. 43); and one to God, "Father, into Thy hands I commit My spirit" (v. 46).

To the very end, words of mercy, hope, and trust flow from His lips.

### *Darkness and Death*

As if He hasn't endured enough pain, people start pounding verbal spikes into His heart. From the Jewish rulers: "He saved others; let Him save Himself if this is the Christ of God, His Chosen One" (v. 35). From the soldiers, who read the inscription above His head: "If You are the King of the Jews, save Yourself!" (v. 37). From the unrepentant thief suffering beside Him: "Are you not the Christ? Save Yourself and us!" (v. 39).

3. W. Phillip Keller, *Rabboni* (Old Tappan, N.J.: Fleming H. Revell Co., Power Books, 1977), pp. 268–69.

Of course, Jesus can save Himself, but He chooses to save the world instead. So, hour after hour, He endures the pain, the insults, the abandonment of His own people. Only once is it almost too much to bear—when His Father abandons Him.

About the sixth hour, noon, darkness falls "over the whole land until the ninth hour" (v. 44). A black veil of mourning covers the sun's face as God lays the combined evil of all the world's sin on Jesus' shoulders. Then He turns away from His own Son. Jesus must drain the dregs of God's judgment alone.

By about the ninth hour, 3 o'clock, Jesus can endure the separation no longer. He screams,

> "Eli, Eli, lama sabachthani?" that is, "My God, My God, why hast Thou forsaken Me?" (Matt. 27:46)

The Father pours out the full measure of His wrath on His precious Lamb—the wrath that we deserve. With a mighty ripping sound, the heavy veil in the temple, which has separated people from God's holy, intimate presence for centuries, tears in two, signifying that the way is now clear for sinners to reach their God (Luke 23:45). Committing His spirit into the loving hands that crushed Him, Jesus breathes His last (v. 46).

## A Concluding Thought

When we consider the price our Lord paid to ransom our captive souls, it causes us to tremble. Such devotion. Such sacrifice. We are left with only one response, really. *Such an extreme price paid for our salvation calls for an extreme commitment*. The kind of commitment Isaac Watts wrote about in "When I Survey the Wondrous Cross."

> When I survey the wondrous cross
> On which the Prince of glory died,
> My richest gain I count but loss,
> And pour contempt on all my pride.
>
> See, from His head, His hands, His feet,
> Sorrow and love flow mingled down:
> Did e'er such love and sorrow meet,
> Or thorns compose so rich a crown?
>
> Were the whole realm of nature mine,
> That were a present far too small;

Love so amazing, so divine,
Demands my soul, my life, my all.[4]

## *Living Insights* STUDY ONE

To die on a cross is to die in shame.

Even the Romans believed it to be "a most cruel and disgusting punishment."[5] To the Jews, it was particularly vile. They categorized crucifixion with hanging, applying Deuteronomy 21:23 to both: "Anyone who is hung on a tree is under God's curse" (NIV).[6]

No right-thinking person would give honor to a man who died as a criminal in disgrace on a cross—much less worship Him. Yet early Christians saw something in Jesus and the Cross that others missed. According to 1 Corinthians 1:18–23, what did they see?

______________________________________________

______________________________________________

How does Paul explain the message of the Cross in Galatians 3:10–14?

______________________________________________

______________________________________________

______________________________________________

Through Christ's disgrace, God poured out grace on us. It's a crazy, foolish, wonderful paradox—one that causes the creatures in heaven to lift their voices in praise (see Rev. 5:9–14). We've provided you some space to write out your own words of praise to the One who suffered and died for you.

______________________________________________

______________________________________________

4. Isaac Watts, "When I Survey the Wondrous Cross," in *Hymns for the Family of God* (Nashville, Tenn.: Paragon Associates, 1976), no. 258.

5. Cicero, as quoted by John R. W. Stott in *The Cross of Christ* (Downers Grove, Ill.: InterVarsity Press, 1986), p. 24.

6. See Stott, *The Cross of Christ*, p. 24.

## *Living Insights* STUDY TWO

As we meditate on the Cross, one question inevitably wells up within us . . . why? Why the beating and scourging and mocking? Why the thorns? Why the nails? Why the utter indignity? Was all that necessary?

Yes . . . to display sin's true and ugly face.

> The crucifixion of Christ was the crowning sin of our race. In his death we shall find all the sins of mankind uniting in foul conspiracy. Envy and pride and hate are there, with covetousness, falsehood, and blasphemy, eager to rush on to cruelty, revenge, and murder. As all the rivers run into the sea, and as all the clouds empty themselves upon the earth, so did all the crimes of man gather to the slaying of the Son of God.[7]

The sum of our sins was accounted for at the Cross, and Jesus bore them all. There was no wrong that Jesus did not make right. There was no darkness that He did not make light. Oh, sinner, if you think you have committed an evil that Jesus cannot forgive, you have not been to the Cross.

Just now, pour out your guilt and shame at His feet. He has seen your worst and accepted you a long time ago.

7. Charles Spurgeon, *Spurgeon at His Best*, comp. Tom Carter (Grand Rapids, Mich.: Baker Book House, 1988), p. 47.

# The Trials of Jesus Christ

| Trial | Officiating Authority | Scripture | Accusation | Legality | Type | Result |
|---|---|---|---|---|---|---|
| 1 | Annas, ex-high priest of the Jews (A.D. 6–15). | John 18:13–23 | Trumped-up charges of irreverence to Annas. | ILLEGAL! Held at night. No specific charges. Prejudice. Violence. | Jewish and Religious | Found guilty of irreverence and rushed to Caiaphas. |
| 2 | Caiaphas—Annas' son-in-law—and the Sanhedrin (A.D. 18–36). | Matthew 26:57–68<br>Mark 14:53–65<br>John 18:24 | Claiming to be the Messiah, the Son of God—blasphemy (worthy of death under Jewish law). | ILLEGAL! Held at night. False witnesses. Prejudice. Violence. | Jewish and Religious | Declared guilty of blasphemy and rushed to the Sanhedrin (Jewish supreme court). |
| 3 | The Sanhedrin—seventy ruling men of Israel (their verdict was needed before He could be taken to Roman officials). | Mark 15:1a<br>Luke 22:66–71 | Claiming to be the Son of God—blasphemy. | ILLEGAL! Accusation switched. No witnesses. Improper voting. | Jewish and Religious | Declared guilty of blasphemy and rushed to Roman official, Pilate. |
| 4 | Pilate, governor of Judea, who was already in "hot water" with Rome (A.D. 26–36). | Matthew 27:11–14<br>Mark 15:1b–5<br>Luke 23:1–7<br>John 18:28–38 | Treason (accusation was changed, since treason was worthy of capital punishment in Rome). | ILLEGAL! Christ was kept under arrest, although He was found innocent. No defense attorney. Violence. | Roman and Civil | Found innocent . . . but rushed to Herod Antipas; mob overruled Pilate. |
| 5 | Herod Antipas, governor of Galilee (4 B.C.–A.D. 39). | Luke 23:8–12 | No accusation was made. | ILLEGAL! No grounds. Mockery in courtroom. No defense attorney. Violence. | Roman and Civil | Mistreated and mocked; returned to Pilate without decision made by Herod. |
| 6 | Pilate (second time). | Matthew 27:15–26<br>Mark 15:6–15<br>Luke 23:18–25<br>John 18:39–19:16 | Treason, though not proven (Pilate bargained with the mob, putting Christ on a level with Barabbas, a criminal). | ILLEGAL! Without proof of guilt, Pilate allowed an innocent man to be condemned. | Roman and Civil | Found innocent, but Pilate "washed his hands" and allowed Him to be crucified. |

Chapter 15

# UP FROM THE GRAVE HE AROSE

*Luke 23:47–24:12*

> And Jesus, crying out with a loud voice, said, "Father, into Thy hands I commit My spirit." And having said this, He breathed His last. (Luke 23:46)

With a deep sigh, Jesus released a final breath into the darkened sky. His head bowed forward. His body slumped.

Jesus was dead.

At least, that was what the people saw. Had the curtain of the spirit world been pulled back, however, they would have seen His soul breaking loose from His body like a ray of sun bursting through the black clouds.

Into the unseen world Jesus soared in a triumphant flight of freedom—no longer tethered to His earthly body, no longer confined to His prison of pain. With unbridled joy, He proclaimed to the spirits that redemption was complete (see 1 Pet. 3:18–19). Salvation had been secured. The price had been paid. It was finished!

Back in the seen world, however, a pall of gloom clung to the hill where His body remained stretched on the cross. To Jesus' enemies, the sight bore a measure of satisfaction; to His friends, despair.

## Reactions to Jesus' Death

In the final verses of chapter 23, Luke isolates four reactions to Jesus' death.

### *A Seasoned Soldier*

The person nearest to Jesus when He died, and the first to respond, was a centurion. As the commander of the crucifixion detail, he had observed many men die on Skull Hill. If they ended up here, they were always the worst sort of men, foaming and snarling with hate.

But Jesus was different. Instead of curses, His lips uttered an offer of forgiveness, a promise of paradise, a heartbreaking cry as a Son to His Father. Watching the way Jesus died must have made the centurion wonder, *Could He be the King they say He is?* Then, when Jesus breathed His last, the physical and spiritual worlds cried out the answer. Matthew tells us in a little more detail what happened:

> And behold, the veil of the temple was torn in two from top to bottom, and the earth shook; and the rocks were split, and the tombs were opened; and many bodies of the saints who had fallen asleep were raised. (Matt. 27:51–52)

The centurion needed no further proof:

> Now when the centurion saw what had happened, he began praising God, saying, "Certainly this man was innocent." (Luke 23:47)

### *The General Public*

From the centurion's praise, Luke's camera next pans to the people scattered around the base of the hill.

> And all the multitudes who came together for this spectacle, when they observed what had happened, began to return, beating their breasts. And all His acquaintances and the women who accompanied Him from Galilee, were standing at a distance, seeing these things. (vv. 48–49)

The lame men and women Jesus had healed, the seekers He had shown the way, the sinners He had forgiven—they all had come to the cross. And when Jesus died, a part of them died too. When it was over, they drifted away, clinging to one another and, Luke says, "beating their breasts"—wailing in unrestrained grief.

Jesus' mother was among the women who watched Him suffer. She heard the thud of the hammer on the spikes. She listened to the chief priests hurl their abuse. She felt her son's pain as only a mother can. Gasping as the spear pierced His side (John 19:34), she must have recalled Simeon's cryptic prophecy—"A sword will pierce even your own soul" (Luke 2:35)—and wept for the boy she once held in her arms.

### *A Believing Council Member*

Joseph of Arimathea is the next person Luke focuses on.

> And behold, a man named Joseph, who was a

> member of the Council, a good and righteous man (he had not consented to their plan and action), a man from Arimathea, a city of the Jews, who was waiting for the kingdom of God; this man went to Pilate and asked for the body of Jesus. And he took it down and wrapped it in a linen cloth, and laid Him in a tomb cut into the rock, where no one had ever lain. And it was the preparation day, and the Sabbath was about to begin. (23:50–54)

John tells us that Nicodemus—also a member of the Council or Sanhedrin—helped Joseph in the difficult task of burial (John 19:38–42).[1] Jewish custom dictated the proper procedure.

> [The body was] usually washed and straightened, and then bandaged tightly from the armpits to the ankles in strips of linen about a foot wide. Aromatic spices, often of a gummy consistency, were placed between the wrappings or folds. They served partially as a preservative and partially as a cement to glue the cloth wrappings into a solid covering. When the body was thus encased, a square piece of cloth was wrapped around the head and tied under the chin to keep the lower jaw from sagging.[2]

Tenderly and solemnly, these two friends of the Lord prepared His body. But they had to move quickly, for the sun was setting. The Sabbath was at hand.

### *A Group of Women*

Lingering behind to help was a caring group of women from Galilee. They followed Nicodemus and Joseph as they carried the body away and

> saw the tomb and how His body was laid. And they returned and prepared spices and perfumes.
>
> And on the Sabbath they rested according to the commandment. (Luke 23:55–56)

1. One question hovers like a dark cloud over these two Council members' act of kindness: Why didn't they stand up for Jesus during His trial before the Sanhedrin? Perhaps they tried, but their dissenting voices were drowned out in the Council's clamor for Jesus' blood.

2. Merrill C. Tenney, *The Reality of the Resurrection* (New York, N.Y.: Harper and Row, Publishers, 1963), p. 117.

Encased in strips of linen, Jesus' body rested in the cool, silent tomb Friday night, all day Saturday, and through the following dark night.

## Reactions to Jesus' Resurrection

Then, in the predawn stillness of Sunday morning, it happened. The miracle of miracles!

### *Material Evidence*

> But on the first day of the week, at early dawn, [the women] came to the tomb, bringing the spices which they had prepared. And they found the stone rolled away from the tomb, but when they entered, they did not find the body of the Lord Jesus. (24:1–3)

The women's minds raced as they tried to make sense of what they saw.

*The stone.* The large, round stone that had been rolled down into a groove in front of the tomb's entrance had been pushed up and out of the way.[3] These stones sometimes weighed a ton or more, and besides, the chief priests and Pharisees had secured a Roman guard for the tomb and "set a seal on the stone" (Matt. 27:62–66). Who could have done this?

*The empty tomb.* Their hearts beating wildly, the women rushed into the burial chamber that had been carved out of the stony hillside. No body! Where could it be?[4]

*The grave clothes.* All that remained were the mummylike wrappings, still molded in the shape of Jesus' body. How could His body be gone and the grave clothes remain intact?

The women searched one another's eyes for answers, but flashes of confusion and fear were all they found.

### *Supernatural Appearance*

> And it happened that while they were perplexed about this, behold, two men suddenly stood near

3. A resurrected body doesn't need stones removed—it can go right through material things (see John 20:19, 26). The stone was removed to let them in so they could see the empty tomb.

4. Skeptics have drawn up three main theories to account for the empty tomb: the women went to the wrong tomb; Jesus only swooned on the cross and escaped under His own power; someone stole the body. However, considering the precautions the religious leaders took to seal and guard the tomb (see Matt. 27:62–66) and the fact that no one has ever been able to produce Jesus' body, resurrection is the only reasonable explanation for the empty tomb.

> them in dazzling apparel; and as the women were terrified and bowed their faces to the ground, the men said to them, "Why do you seek the living One among the dead?" (Luke 24:4–5)

A light exploded; a voice boomed. And the women, Luke tells us, were "terrified." The Greek word comes from a word group with the primary verb *phebomai*, which means "to flee."[5] The kind of panic that sends us running for our lives gripped the women's hearts as they trembled before the angels.

The heavenly beings continued:

> "He is not here, but He has risen. Remember how He spoke to you while He was still in Galilee, saying that the Son of Man must be delivered into the hands of sinful men, and be crucified, and the third day rise again." (vv. 6–7)

### *Personal Responses*

As the rumbling voices faded and the angels' glory dimmed, a light clicked on in the women's minds. Yes! Jesus had risen just as He said He would (see 9:22; 18:32–33).

> And they remembered His words, and returned from the tomb and reported all these things to the eleven and to all the rest. Now they were Mary Magdalene and Joanna and Mary the mother of James; also the other women with them were telling these things to the apostles. (24:8–10)

We can imagine that when the disciples heard the wonderful news, they lit up with joy. . . . Wrong.

> And these words appeared to them as nonsense, and they would not believe them. (v. 11)

Ironically, the first skeptics of the Resurrection were Jesus' own disciples. They thought the story was "nonsense." William Barclay tells us,

> The word used is one employed by Greek medical

5. *Theological Dictionary of the New Testament*, ed. Gerhard Kittel and Gerhard Friedrich, translated and abridged in one volume by Geoffrey W. Bromiley (1985; reprint, Grand Rapids, Mich.: William B. Eerdmans Publishing Co., 1992), p. 1272.

> writers to describe the babbling of a fevered and insane mind.[6]

"You're crazy," the disciples scowled. But Peter, accompanied by John, ran to the tomb to see for himself (see John 20:3–9).

> Stooping and looking in, he saw the linen wrappings only; and he went away to his home, marveling at that which had happened. (Luke 24:12)

It is true, Jesus is alive!

That fact is the pillar upon which all Christian truth rests. Because He is raised, sin can be forgiven. Satan's doom is sealed. Death is not the final conqueror.

Because He is raised, we shall be raised someday. Like Jesus' body, our bodies in their glorified state will burst forth from the grave and be joined to our souls, and we will live with Him forever. What a wonderful hope!

## And Now . . . What Is Your Reaction?

One response to Jesus' death and resurrection remains to be examined—yours. Like the disciples at first, you may shake your head and say it's all nonsense. Before you reach your final verdict, though, consider Paul's compelling argument:

> If Christ has not been raised, your faith is worthless; you are still in your sins. Then those also who have fallen asleep in Christ have perished. If we have hoped in Christ in this life only, we are of all men most to be pitied. (1 Cor. 15:17–19)

To deny the Resurrection is to smash the pillar upon which all Christian hope rests. Thankfully, God has designed it to be a mighty pillar. If your jury is still out concerning the Resurrection, examine the evidence carefully. There is no firmer foundation upon which to build your life . . . or your future.[7]

6. William Barclay, *The Gospel of Luke*, rev. ed., The Daily Study Bible Series (Philadelphia, Pa.: Westminster Press, 1975), p. 292.

7. For further study, see *The Resurrection Factor* by Josh McDowell (San Bernardino, Calif.: Here's Life Publishers, 1981); *Who Moved the Stone*, by Frank Morison (1930; reprint, Grand Rapids, Mich.: Zondervan Publishing House, Lamplighter Books, 1958); *The Reality of the Resurrection*, by Merrill C. Tenney.

## *Living Insights* STUDY ONE

Christ's resurrection is the cornerstone of Christianity. From the following verses, write down the spiritual implications of the empty tomb.

Romans 4:22–25

Romans 8:10–11

1 Thessalonians 4:14

1 Peter 1:3–5

Perhaps the greatest implication of the Resurrection is the assurance that God has a future for us. The multitudes went away "beating their breasts" (Luke 23:48) because they thought their hope had died with Jesus. For all they knew, the final chapter had been written—what could be more final than death? Evil had conquered good. The story was over.

But God had a surprise ending waiting—the same surprise ending that awaits all who believe in Christ. Read Romans 8:35–39. What can you face today, knowing that your future is secure?

## *Living Insights* STUDY TWO

Spend some reflective time with Christ, who won our victory over death. You've already taken in Luke's account of Jesus' resurrection, so now read the accounts of the other gospel writers: Matthew 28:1–15, Mark 16:1–11, John 20:1–18.

Then linger with the Lord in prayer. Perhaps this prayer of Ken Gire's, based on John's Resurrection story, can help guide your thoughts.

> Dear Risen Lord,
>
> How hard it is to see clearly when devastating circumstances fill my eyes with tears. How blurry everything gets. Even you get blurry, and the sound of your voice becomes strangely unfamiliar.
>
> Help me to blink away those tears to see that you are standing beside me, wanting to know why I am crying . . . wanting to know where it hurts . . . wanting to wipe away every tear from my eyes.
>
> Thank you, Jesus, for being there, for never leaving me or forsaking me, even in the darkest and chilliest hours of my life.
>
> From those circumstances that have shrouded my heart and entombed me, I pray that you would roll away the stone. It is too heavy and I am too weak to roll it away myself.
>
> Where there is doubt, roll away the stone and
> resurrect my faith.
> Where there is depression, cast aside the
> grave clothes and release my joy.
> Where there is despair, chase away the night
> and bring a sunrise to my hope.
>
> Yet in my doubt, in my depression, in my despair, help me to continue to love you. Even if I don't understand how you are working in my life.
>
> And I rejoice that no matter how dark the Friday or how cold the tomb, that with you as my risen Savior, there is always the warm hope of an Easter morning. . . .[8]

8. Ken Gire, *Intimate Moments with the Savior* (Grand Rapids, Mich.: Zondervan Publishing House, 1989), p. 133.

Chapter 16

# THE MASTER SAYS FAREWELL TO HIS FRIENDS

*Luke 24:13–53*

One week. It's a rather inconsequential unit of time. Fifty-two of them are packed into a year, thousands into a lifetime. We dispense them without much thought: "I won't be gone too long on vacation, just a week." "Summer's going fast. In a couple of weeks, school starts." "You won't have to wear the bandage very long—a few weeks at the most."

Yet think of the earthshaking events that took place in the space of one week at the end of Jesus' life:

- After His triumphal entry into Jerusalem on Sunday (Luke 19:28–44), He drove the profit-mongers from the temple. Then He spent His first few days in *instruction*, revealing truth to His many followers and debating the religious leaders (chaps. 20 and 21).
- Following this was a period of *preparation*: Judas prepared to betray the Lord, the disciples made the arrangements for the Passover, and Jesus readied His men for the coming conflict (22:1–38).
- A time of *supplication* came next, with Jesus praying feverishly in Gethsemane (vv. 39–46).
- Judas' kiss set in motion the events of the *Crucifixion*, in which Jesus endured six unjust trials and the agony of death on the cross (22:47–23:56).
- Then on Sunday morning came the *Resurrection*—Jesus' glorious triumph over sin and death.

Surely, this was a week like none other—one that remains fixed at the pinnacle of history. And it's not over yet.

## A Lingering Look at the Concluding Scenes

In the Resurrection's afterglow, Luke reveals two surprise appearances of the risen Christ: His commission to His followers to carry the news of His victory to the world, and His ascension.

### *With Two Believers on the Road to Emmaus*

The first scene takes place later the same day the women discovered the empty tomb.

> And behold, two of them were going that very day to a village named Emmaus, which was about seven miles from Jerusalem. And they were conversing with each other about all these things which had taken place. (Luke 24:13–14)

The traumatic wave of recent events has sent these two disciples reeling. Trying desperately to sort through the splintered debris of their faith, they leave the city.

Jesus, though, steps into their confusion and heartache in a most natural way—without terrifying bursts of light, without booming announcements. Gently, He probes their pain.

> And it came about that while they were conversing and discussing, Jesus Himself approached, and began traveling with them. But their eyes were prevented from recognizing Him. And He said to them, "What are these words that you are exchanging with one another as you are walking?" And they stood still, looking sad. And one of them, named Cleopas, answered and said to Him, "Are You the only one visiting Jerusalem and unaware of the things which have happened here in these days?" And He said to them, "What things?" (vv. 15–19a)

How like Jesus not to barge in with all the answers but ask a question and listen to the other person's perspective of the situation (see also 9:18; 10:26, 36; 14:3, 5; 18:41). He certainly draws out an answer from Cleopas and his friend.

> And they said to Him, "The things about Jesus the Nazarene, who was a prophet mighty in deed and word in the sight of God and all the people, and how the chief priests and our rulers delivered Him up to the sentence of death, and crucified Him. But we were hoping that it was He who was going to redeem Israel. Indeed, besides all this, it is the third day since these things happened. But also some women among us amazed us. When they were at the

> tomb early in the morning, and did not find His body, they came, saying that they had also seen a vision of angels, who said that He was alive. And some of those who were with us went to the tomb and found it just exactly as the women also had said; but Him they did not see." (24:19b–24)

Like a father who pretends to forget his child's pined-for present, then unveils it at the last minute, so Jesus must have ached to reveal His identity to these two. But He keeps the surprise behind His back until He can explain to them the crucial meaning of the cross and the empty tomb.

> And He said to them, "O foolish men and slow of heart to believe in all that the prophets have spoken! Was it not necessary for the Christ to suffer these things and to enter into His glory?" And beginning with Moses and with all the prophets, He explained to them the things concerning Himself in all the Scriptures. (vv. 25–27)

Wouldn't we love to have been there for that sermon! Beginning with Genesis, Jesus threads the scarlet truth of redemption all the way through the Old Testament, weaving a tapestry of both suffering and glory for the Messiah. It might have looked something like this:

> In Genesis, He is the Seed of the woman.
> In Exodus, the Passover Lamb.
> In Leviticus, the atoning sacrifice.
> In Numbers, the bronze serpent.
> In Deuteronomy, the promised Prophet.
> In Joshua, the Captain of the Lord's host.
> In Judges, the Deliverer.
> In Ruth, the heavenly Kinsman.
> In the books of Samuel, Kings, and Chronicles, the promised King.
> In Ezra and Nehemiah, the Restorer of the nation.
> In Esther, the Advocate.
> In Job, the Redeemer.
> In Psalms, the All in All.
> In Proverbs, the Pattern.
> In Ecclesiastes, the Goal.
> In Song of Solomon, the Beloved.

In the prophets, the coming Prince of Peace.[1]

As Jesus shows this and more to the two disciples, truth flashes in the darkness of their despair. Soon a flame of hope ignites. By the time they reach Emmaus, their hearts are ablaze.

Eager to hear more, they urge Jesus not to go farther, "Stay with us" (v. 29). They sit down for a meal, and Jesus takes the bread, blesses it, breaks it, and gives it to them (v. 30). Perhaps the scene of Jesus multiplying the loaves suddenly replays in their minds (see 9:14–17). Or maybe, for the first time that evening, they notice the nail scars in His hands. Whatever the trigger God used, He chose this moment to open their eyes,

> and they recognized Him; and He vanished from their sight. And they said to one another, "Were not our hearts burning within us while He was speaking to us on the road, while He was explaining the Scriptures to us?" And they arose that very hour and returned to Jerusalem, and found gathered together the eleven and those who were with them, saying, "The Lord has really risen, and has appeared to Simon."[2] (24:31–35)

### *With Eleven Disciples in Several Settings*

*First appearance and conversation.* The two disciples barely finish their account when Jesus surprises all of them with another visit.

> And while they were telling these things, He Himself stood in their midst. But they were startled and frightened and thought that they were seeing a spirit. (vv. 36–37)

No wonder they think He's a ghost—they've never seen a glorified body before. No one has, for Jesus is the first fruits to fall off a vine that will one day produce a bumper crop of resurrected believers (1 Cor. 15:20, 22).

1. Adapted from the study guide *A Look at the Book*, coauthored by Lee Hough and Bryce Klabunde, from the Bible-teaching ministry of Charles R. Swindoll (Anaheim, Calif.: Insight for Living, 1994), pp. 18–19. Based on J. B. Fowler, Jr., *Illustrating Great Words of the New Testament* (Nashville, Tenn.: Broadman Press, 1991), p. 98.

2. Before the two from Emmaus could relate their story, the Eleven reported to them that Simon had also seen the risen Lord (see 1 Cor. 15:5). Luke doesn't record the details of this appearance.

> And He said to them, "Why are you troubled, and why do doubts arise in your hearts? See My hands and My feet, that it is I Myself; touch Me and see, for a spirit does not have flesh and bones as you see that I have." [And when He had said this, He showed them His hands and His feet.] And while they still could not believe it for joy and were marveling, He said to them, "Have you anything here to eat?" And they gave Him a piece of a broiled fish; and He took it and ate it before them. (Luke 24:38–43)

That's proof positive! Jesus is real—just as real as the promise of our own resurrection. When He returns, He will raise our mortal bodies and clothe us in immortality (1 Cor. 15:50–53). We will be like Him: not limited by the natural laws of gravity, space, and time, yet able to eat and feel and fellowship with one another. (1 John 3:2)

*Next appearance and commission.* The verses that follow probably record later events, as Luke skips ahead forty days to Jesus' final appearance to His disciples (compare Acts 1:3). In this visit, the Lord again emphasizes that His story is told throughout the Scriptures.

> Now He said to them, "These are My words which I spoke to you while I was still with you, that all things which are written about Me in the Law of Moses and the Prophets and the Psalms must be fulfilled." Then He opened their minds to understand the Scriptures, and He said to them, "Thus it is written, that the Christ should suffer and rise again from the dead the third day." (Luke 24:44–46)

How important it is that in our study and application of the Bible we don't miss the central and most important point—Christ Himself.

Second, Jesus charges His followers to proclaim the gospel, showing them from the Scriptures

> "that repentance for forgiveness of sins should be proclaimed in [My] name to all the nations, beginning from Jerusalem. You are witnesses of these things." (vv. 47–48)

Then, in His last words recorded in Luke's gospel, He makes a promise:

> "And behold, I am sending forth the promise of My

> Father upon you; but you are to stay in the city until you are clothed with power from on high." (v. 49)

This would be stunningly fulfilled in Acts 2.

*Final appearance and Ascension.* Leading His dear friends out of Jerusalem, Jesus backtracks the route of His triumphal entry, going up the Mount of Olives to Bethany (Luke 24:50a). Here He will make His triumphal exit out of the earthly sphere in which He was born thirty-three years before and into the courts of His celestial home.

As Jesus lifts His hands toward heaven, He blesses His disciples, laying on their shoulders His mantle of ministry (v. 50b). Then He rises into the sky and the clouds receive Him into heaven (see Acts 1:9). Luke states it simply, "He parted from them" (Luke 24:51).

As the following chart illustrates, Jesus' farewell is both an ending and a beginning—a sad sunset and the thrilling dawn of a new day for Jesus and His followers.

| *The Ascension: An Ending* | *The Ascension: A Beginning* |
|---|---|
| They no longer see Jesus on earth. | They have to start walking by faith and not by sight. |
| They no longer feel the physical comfort of His presence. | Jesus ministers to them in new ways: He will intercede on their behalf before God (Rom. 8:34) and send the Holy Spirit to empower them (Acts 1:8). |
| His mission to atone for the sins of the world is finished. | His ministry as their advocate against Satan's accusations is just beginning (1 John 2:1). |
| His descent into the depths of human limitations and suffering is over. | In His glorified body, He begins a new relationship with the Father and the angels that will continue forever. |

Jesus is the first to enter God's throne room in a glorified, resurrected human body. When He stepped into heaven and took His seat at the right hand of the Father, the angels' voices must have exploded in praise. He has won the victory! They can see His side and feet and hands that still bear the scars of the battle. He will wear these marks for eternity as proof that the price for our sins has been paid with His blood.

Luke fittingly concludes His story of Jesus' life with the praise of the disciples, as they anticipate the next chapter—the coming of the Holy Spirit:

> And they returned to Jerusalem with great joy, and were continually in the temple, praising God. (Luke 24:52–53)

## A Personal Response to the Living Christ

As we reflect on the scenes of Jesus appearing to the two men on the road to Emmaus and to the Eleven, a couple of principles emerge.

First, *there are times when Jesus comes near.* Like Cleopas and his companion, we may be walking down a road of doubt and confusion. Questions rain down faster than we find answers to deflect them. Suddenly, unpretentiously, Jesus falls in step with us bearing a calming reminder from Scripture. We invite Him, "Stay with me through this," and we feel His presence.

Second, *there are other times when He seems far away.* It's not that He abandons us. Rather, He reminds us that He is high and lifted up. He is the glorified Son of God. Though His position at the Father's right hand may make Him seem distant, it is from there that He blesses "us with every spiritual blessing" (Eph. 1:3). When we see Him as He is, we can only respond as the disciples did and keep on praising Him until He comes.

Perhaps Spurgeon's words will help us with our praise.

> I like to think of our Lord's ascension in this simple but sublime manner. I might have been terrified if I had been Elisha walking with Elijah when the horses of fire and the chariots of fire came to take him away, but there was nothing terrible about this ascension of Christ. He was not a prophet of fire; He was gentle, meek, and lowly, and there was nothing to inspire terror in the way He ascended to heaven. It is, to my mind, very beautiful to think of there being no medium employed in connection with His ascension, no angels' wings to bear Him upward, no visible arm of omnipotence to lift Him gently from the earth. . . . No; but He rises by His own power and majesty; He needs no help. Glad would the angels have been to come once more to earth as they had

> come at His birth, as they had come to the wilderness, as they had come to His tomb—gladly would they have ministered to Him; but He needed not their ministry. . . . He proved the innate power of His Deity, by which He could depart out of the world just when He willed, breaking the law of gravitation, and suspending the laws usually governing matter. . . . "A cloud received Him out of their sight," for I suppose they had then seen all that they ought to see; and, perhaps, behind that cloud there were scenes of glory which it was not possible for human eyes to gaze upon, and words which it was not lawful for human beings to hear.[3]

"Blessed be the Lord God of Israel, For He has visited us and accomplished redemption for His people" (Luke 1:68)!

## *Living Insights* STUDY ONE

William Barclay draws upon the story of the two travelers on the road to Emmaus to highlight a precious quality of our Lord's.

> [The story] tells us of the ability of Jesus to make sense of things. The whole situation seemed to these two men to have no explanation. Their hopes and dreams were shattered. There is all the poignant, wistful, bewildered regret in the world in their sorrowing words, "We were hoping that he was the one who was going to rescue Israel." They were the words of men whose hopes were dead and buried. Then Jesus came and talked with them, and the meaning of life became clear and the darkness became light. A story-teller makes one of his characters say to the one with whom he has fallen in love, "I never knew what life meant until I saw it in your eyes." It is only in Jesus that, even in the bewildering times, we learn what life means.[4]

3. Charles Haddon Spurgeon, *The Treasury of the Bible*, volume 6, Luke 15:8 to Romans 3:25 (reprint; Grand Rapids, Mich.: Baker Book House, 1981), p. 217.

4. William Barclay, *The Gospel of Luke*, rev. ed., The Daily Study Bible Series (Philadelphia, Pa.: Westminster Press, 1975), p. 295.

Have you been wandering down an Emmaus road, trying to piece together a shattered dream? Groping for answers but only finding more questions? If so, describe the darkness that is troubling you.

___

___

___

Wouldn't it be wonderful for Christ Himself to page through the Scriptures with you to show you the way back to Jerusalem and to hope? We may not have His physical presence, but we do have the Holy Spirit. Perhaps, in your search for answers, you've forgotten to look to the Source of all knowledge. Take a few moments to ask for the Spirit's wisdom as you look to the Bible for help. Perhaps He'll guide you to a psalm or a proverb or a verse in one of the epistles. Wherever He takes you, my prayer for you is this:

> That the God of our Lord Jesus Christ, the Father of glory, may give to you a spirit of wisdom and of revelation in the knowledge of Him. I pray that the eyes of your heart may be enlightened, so that you may know what is the hope of His calling, what are the riches of the glory of His inheritance in the saints, and what is the surpassing greatness of His power toward us who believe. (Eph. 1:17–19a)

To what Scripture did the Spirit lead you, and what did you learn?

___

___

___

___

## *Living Insights* — STUDY TWO

For centuries, people have been captivated by Leonardo da Vinci's Mona Lisa. Intrigued by her enigmatic expression, some gaze at her for hours. What is she thinking? What is behind her demure smile? Mona Lisa is more than just a work of art; she is a person with dreams and loves and secrets.

Through four volumes of study, we have gazed into Luke's portrait of Jesus. We've peered into the eyes of our Savior and studied His passions. We've seen His broad smile as He welcomed the children, and we have winced at His agonizing grimace on the cross. Jesus is more than just a historical figure; He's a person who invites us to know Him intimately.

In this final Living Insight, we've provided you some space to ponder the face of the Savior one last time before setting down this fourth volume. What have you seen in Him that you never saw before? How has He become more real to you? What changes has He made in your life?

**Lingering over the Savior's Face**

# Books for Probing Further

If Luke were here to jot down a parting word of advice for us, what would he say? I think he'd write something like this: build your life on Christ, not a system of religion. The following poem by John Oxenham echoes that advice.

**Credo**

Not what, but *Whom*, I do believe,
  That, in my darkest hour of need,
  Hath comfort that no mortal creed
  To mortal man may give;—
Not what, but *Whom!*
  For Christ is more than all the creeds,
  And his full life of gentle deeds
  Shall all the creeds outlive.
Not what I do believe, but *Whom!*
  *Who* walks beside me in the gloom?
  *Who* shares the burden wearisome?
  *Who* all the dim way doth illume,
  And bids me look beyond the tomb
  The larger life to live?—
Not what I do believe,
  But *Whom!*
  Not what
  But *Whom!*[1]

Below are a few books that will help you lay the foundation of your life on the "Whom" of the Bible, the Savior of the world.

Gire, Ken. *Intense Moments with the Savior: Learning to Feel*. Grand Rapids, Mich.: Zondervan Publishing House, 1994.

Lucado, Max. *And the Angels Were Silent*. Portland, Oreg.: Multnomah Press, 1992.

1. John Oxenham, "Credo," in *Christ in Poetry*, comp. and ed. Thomas Curtis Clark and Hazel Davis Clark (New York, N.Y.: Association Press, 1952), pp. 342–43.

———. *No Wonder They Call Him the Savior*. Portland, Oreg.: Multnomah Press, 1986.

———. *Six Hours One Friday*. Portland, Oreg.: Multnomah Press, 1989.

Rosen, Ceil and Moishe. *Christ in the Passover*. Chicago, Ill.: Moody Press, 1978.

Stott, John R. W. *The Cross of Christ*. Downers Grove, Ill.: InterVarsity Press, 1986.

Wilcock, Michael. *The Message of Luke*. The Bible Speaks Today series. Downers Grove, Ill.: InterVarsity Press, 1979.

Some of these books may be out of print and available only through a library. For those currently available, please contact your local Christian bookstore. Books by Charles R. Swindoll may be obtained through Insight for Living. IFL also offers some books by other authors—please note the ordering information that follows and contact the office that serves you.

# Ordering Information

## The Consummation of Something Miraculous

### Cassette Tapes and Study Guide

This Bible study guide was designed to be used independently or in conjunction with the broadcast of Chuck Swindoll's taped messages which are listed below. If you would like to order cassette tapes or further copies of this study guide, please see the information given below and the order forms provided at the end of this guide.

| | | U.S. | Canada |
|---|---|---|---|
| CSM | Study guide | $ 4.95 ea. | $ 6.50 ea. |
| CSMCS | Cassette series, includes all individual tapes, album cover, and one complimentary study guide | 52.75 | 61.75 |
| CSM 1–8 | Individual cassettes, includes messages A and B | 6.00 ea. | 7.48 ea. |

The prices are subject to change without notice.

CSM 1-A: *The Subject Everybody Ignores*—Luke 16:19–31
B: *How Not to Be a Stumbling Block*—Luke 17:1–19

CSM 2-A: *Knowing Where You Are . . . Knowing Where You're Going*—Luke 17:20–37
B: *You Want to Be Godly? Start Here*—Luke 18:1–17

CSM 3-A: *Rich Man, Poor Man, Son of Man . . . Me*—Luke 18:18–43
B: *Seeking the Sinner, Saving the Lost*—Luke 19:1–10

CSM 4-A: *Making Sense with Your Dollars*—Luke 19:11–27
B: *Unforgettable Scenes of the Savior*—Luke 19:28–48

CSM 5-A: *Fighting Fire with Fire*—Luke 20:1–26
B: *His Best . . . for Our Good*—Luke 20:27–47

CSM 6-A: *Lifting the Prophetic Veil*—Luke 21
B: *Strong Leadership in Stormy Times*—Luke 22:1–30

CSM 7-A: *The Darkest of All Nights*—Luke 22:31–62
B: *The Day Christ Died*—Luke 22:63–23:46

CSM 8-A: *Up from the Grave He Arose*—Luke 23:47–24:12
B: *The Master Says Farewell to His Friends*—Luke 24:13–53

## How to Order by Phone or FAX

(Credit card orders only)

**United States:** 1-800-772-8888 from 7:00 A.M. to 4:30 P.M., Pacific time, Monday through Friday
FAX (714) 575-5496 anytime, day or night

Canada: 1-800-663-7639, Vancouver residents call (604) 532-7172 from 8:00 A.M. to 5:00 P.M., Pacific time, Monday through Friday
FAX (604) 532-7173 anytime, day or night

**Australia and the South Pacific:** (03) 9-872-4606 or FAX (03) 9-874-8890 from 8:00 A.M. to 5:00 P.M., Monday through Friday

**Other International Locations:** call the Ordering Services Department in the United States at (714) 575-5000 during the hours listed above.

## How to Order by Mail

**United States**

- Mail to: Processing Services Department
  Insight for Living
  Post Office Box 69000
  Anaheim, CA 92817-0900
- Sales tax: California residents add 7.25%.
- Shipping and handling charges must be added to each order. See chart on order form for amount.
- Payment: personal checks, money orders, credit cards (Visa, MasterCard, Discover Card, and American Express). No invoices or COD orders available.
- $10 fee for *any* returned check.

Canada

- Mail to: Insight for Living Ministries
  Post Office Box 2510
  Vancouver, BC V6B 3W7
- Sales tax: please add 7% GST. British Columbia residents also add 7% sales tax (on tapes or cassette series).
- Shipping and handling charges must be added to each order. See chart on order form for amount.

• Payment: personal cheques, money orders, credit cards (Visa, Master-Card). No invoices or COD orders available.
• Delivery: approximately four weeks.

---

**Australia and the South Pacific**
• Mail to: Insight for Living, Inc.
GPO Box 2823 EE
Melbourne, Victoria 3001, Australia
• Shipping: add 25% to the total order.
• Delivery: approximately four to six weeks.
• Payment: personal checks payable in Australian funds, international money orders, or credit cards (Visa, MasterCard, and BankCard).

---

**Other International Locations**
• Mail to: Processing Services Department
Insight for Living
Post Office Box 69000
Anaheim, CA 92817-0900
• Shipping and delivery time: please see chart that follows.
• Payment: personal checks payable in U.S. funds, international money orders, or credit cards (Visa, MasterCard, and American Express).

| *Type of Shipping* | *Postage Cost* | *Delivery* |
|---|---|---|
| Surface | 10% of total order* | 6 to 10 weeks |
| Airmail | 25% of total order* | under 6 weeks |

**Use U.S. price as a base.*

## Our Guarantee

Your complete satisfaction is our top priority here at Insight for Living. If you're not completely satisfied with anything you order, please return it for full credit, a refund, or a replacement, as *you* prefer.

## Insight for Living Catalog

The Insight for Living catalog features study guides, tapes, and books by a variety of Christian authors. To obtain a free copy, call us at the numbers listed above.

# Order Form

## United States, Australia, and Other International Locations

(Canadian residents please use order form on reverse side.)

CSMCS represents the entire *Consummation of Something Miraculous* series in a special album cover, while CSM 1–8 are the individual tapes included in the series. CSM represents this study guide, should you desire to order additional copies.

| | | |
|---|---|---|
| **CSM** | **Study guide** | **$ 4.95 ea.** |
| **CSMCS** | **Cassette series, includes all individual tapes, album cover, and one complimentary study guide** | **52.75** |
| **CSM 1–8** | **Individual cassettes, includes messages A and B** | **6.00 ea.** |

| Product Code | Product Description | Quantity | Unit Price | Total |
|---|---|---|---|---|
| | | | $ | $ |
| | | | | |

| | |
|---|---|
| **Subtotal** | |
| **California Residents—Sales Tax** *Add 7.25% of subtotal.* | |
| **UPS ❑ First Class ❑** *Shipping and handling must be added. See chart for charges.* | |
| **Non-United States Residents** *Australia add 25%. All other locations: U.S. price plus 10% surface postage or 25% airmail.* | |
| **Gift to Insight for Living** *Tax-deductible in the United States.* | |
| **Total Amount Due** *Please do not send cash.* | $ |

| *Amount of Order* | *First Class* | *UPS* |
|---|---|---|
| $ 7.50 and under | 1.00 | 4.00 |
| $ 7.51 to 12.50 | 1.50 | 4.25 |
| $12.51 to 25.00 | 3.50 | 4.50 |
| $25.01 to 35.00 | 4.50 | 4.75 |
| $35.01 to 60.00 | 5.50 | 5.25 |
| $60.00 and over | 6.50 | 5.75 |

Fed Ex and Fourth Class are also available. Please call for details.

*Prices are subject to change without notice.*

**Payment by:** ❑ Check or money order payable to Insight for Living ❑ Credit card

(Circle one): Visa MasterCard Discover Card American Express BankCard (In Australia)

Number ____________________

Expiration Date __________ Signature ____________________

*We cannot process your credit card purchase without your signature.*

Name ____________________

Address ____________________

City ____________________ State __________

Zip Code __________ Country ____________________

Telephone (      ) ____________________ Radio Station ___ ___ ___ ___

*If questions arise concerning your order, we may need to contact you.*

**Mail this order form to the Processing Services Department at one of these addresses:**

**Insight for Living**
Post Office Box 69000, Anaheim, CA 92817-0900

**Insight for Living, Inc.**
GPO Box 2823 EE, Melbourne, VIC 3001, Australia

# Order Form
## Canadian Residents

(Residents of the United States, Australia, and other international locations, please use order form on reverse side.)

CSMCS represents the entire *Consummation of Something Miraculous* series in a special album cover, while CSM 1–8 are the individual tapes included in the series. CSM represents this study guide, should you desire to order additional copies.

| | | |
|---|---|---|
| **CSM** | **Study guide** | **$ 6.50 ea.** |
| **CSMCS** | **Cassette series, includes all individual tapes, album cover, and one complimentary study guide** | **61.75** |
| **CSM 1–8** | **Individual cassettes, includes messages A and B** | **7.48 ea.** |

| Product Code | Product Description | Quantity | Unit Price | Total |
|---|---|---|---|---|
| | | | $ | $ |
| | | | | |
| | | | **Subtotal** | |
| | | | **Add 7% GST** | |
| | | | **British Columbia Residents** *Add 7% sales tax on individual tapes or cassette series.* | |
| | | | **Shipping** *Shipping and handling must be added. See chart for charges.* | |
| | | | **Gift to Insight for Living Ministries** *Tax-deductible in Canada.* | |
| | | | **Total Amount Due** *Please do not send cash.* | $ |

| *Amount of Order* | *Canada Post* |
|---|---|
| Orders to $10.00 | 2.00 |
| $10.01 to 30.00 | 3.50 |
| $30.01 to 50.00 | 5.00 |
| $50.01 to 99.99 | 7.00 |
| $100 and over | Free |

Loomis is also available. Please call for details.

*Prices are subject to change without notice.*

**Payment by:** ❑ Cheque or money order payable to Insight for Living Ministries
❑ Credit card

(Circle one): Visa MasterCard Number____________________

Expiration Date________ Signature____________________

*We cannot process your credit card purchase without your signature.*

Name____________________

Address____________________

City____________________ Province________

Postal Code__________ Country__________

Telephone (     )________________ Radio Station___ ___ ___ ___

*If questions arise concerning your order, we may need to contact you.*

**Mail this order form to the Processing Services Department at the following address:**

**Insight for Living Ministries**
Post Office Box 2510
Vancouver, BC, Canada V6B 3W7

# Order Form

## United States, Australia, and Other International Locations

(Canadian residents please use order form on reverse side.)

CSMCS represents the entire *Consummation of Something Miraculous* series in a special album cover, while CSM 1–8 are the individual tapes included in the series. CSM represents this study guide, should you desire to order additional copies.

| | | |
|---|---|---|
| **CSM** | **Study guide** | **$ 4.95 ea.** |
| **CSMCS** | **Cassette series, includes all individual tapes, album cover, and one complimentary study guide** | **52.75** |
| **CSM 1–8** | **Individual cassettes, includes messages A and B** | **6.00 ea.** |

| Product Code | Product Description | Quantity | Unit Price | Total |
|---|---|---|---|---|
| | | | $ | $ |
| | | | | |

| | |
|---|---|
| **Subtotal** | |
| **California Residents—Sales Tax** *Add 7.25% of subtotal.* | |
| **UPS ❑ First Class ❑** *Shipping and handling must be added. See chart for charges.* | |
| **Non-United States Residents** *Australia add 25%. All other locations: U.S. price plus 10% surface postage or 25% airmail.* | |
| **Gift to Insight for Living** *Tax-deductible in the United States.* | |
| **Total Amount Due** *Please do not send cash.* | $ |

| *Amount of Order* | *First Class* | *UPS* |
|---|---|---|
| $ 7.50 and under | 1.00 | 4.00 |
| $ 7.51 to 12.50 | 1.50 | 4.25 |
| $12.51 to 25.00 | 3.50 | 4.50 |
| $25.01 to 35.00 | 4.50 | 4.75 |
| $35.01 to 60.00 | 5.50 | 5.25 |
| $60.00 and over | 6.50 | 5.75 |

Fed Ex and Fourth Class are also available. Please call for details.

*Prices are subject to change without notice.*

**Payment by:** ❑ Check or money order payable to Insight for Living ❑ Credit card

(Circle one): Visa MasterCard Discover Card American Express BankCard (In Australia)

Number ______________________________

Expiration Date __________ Signature ______________________________

*We cannot process your credit card purchase without your signature.*

Name ______________________________

Address ______________________________

City ______________________________ State __________

Zip Code ______________ Country ______________________________

Telephone (    ) ______________________ Radio Station ____ ____ ____ ____

*If questions arise concerning your order, we may need to contact you.*

**Mail this order form to the Processing Services Department at one of these addresses:**

**Insight for Living**
Post Office Box 69000, Anaheim, CA 92817-0900

**Insight for Living, Inc.**
GPO Box 2823 EE, Melbourne, VIC 3001, Australia

ECFA MEMBER EVANGELICAL COUNCIL FOR FINANCIAL ACCOUNTABILITY

# Order Form

## Canadian Residents

(Residents of the United States, Australia, and other international locations, please use order form on reverse side.)

CSMCS represents the entire *Consummation of Something Miraculous* series in a special album cover, while CSM 1–8 are the individual tapes included in the series. CSM represents this study guide, should you desire to order additional copies.

| | | |
|---|---|---|
| **CSM** | **Study guide** | **$ 6.50 ea.** |
| **CSMCS** | **Cassette series, includes all individual tapes, album cover, and one complimentary study guide** | **61.75** |
| **CSM 1–8** | **Individual cassettes, includes messages A and B** | **7.48 ea.** |

| Product Code | Product Description | Quantity | Unit Price | Total |
|---|---|---|---|---|
| | | | $ | $ |
| | | | | |

| *Amount of Order* | *Canada Post* |
|---|---|
| Orders to $10.00 | 2.00 |
| $10.01 to 30.00 | 3.50 |
| $30.01 to 50.00 | 5.00 |
| $50.01 to 99.99 | 7.00 |
| $100 and over | Free |

Loomis is also available. Please call for details.

| | |
|---|---|
| **Subtotal** | |
| **Add 7% GST** | |
| **British Columbia Residents** *Add 7% sales tax on individual tapes or cassette series.* | |
| **Shipping** *Shipping and handling must be added. See chart for charges.* | |
| **Gift to Insight for Living Ministries** *Tax-deductible in Canada.* | |
| **Total Amount Due** *Please do not send cash.* | $ |

*Prices are subject to change without notice.*

**Payment by:** ❑ Cheque or money order payable to Insight for Living Ministries
❑ Credit card

(Circle one): Visa MasterCard Number________________________

Expiration Date__________ Signature________________________

*We cannot process your credit card purchase without your signature.*

Name________________________________________

Address______________________________________

City____________________________ Province__________

Postal Code______________ Country____________________

Telephone (      )__________________ Radio Station____ ____ ____ ____

*If questions arise concerning your order, we may need to contact you.*

**Mail this order form to the Processing Services Department at the following address:**

**Insight for Living Ministries**
Post Office Box 2510
Vancouver, BC, Canada V6B 3W7